MW01712220

SYMBOLS AND THEIR MEANINGS

SYMBOLS AND THEIR MEANINGS

JACK TRESIDDER

BARNES & NOBLE
NEW YORK

Symbols and their Meanings
Jack Tresidder

This 2006 edition published by Metro Books, by arrangement with Duncan Baird Publishers

Managing Editor: Judy Dean
Picture research: Julia Brown
Edited and designed by cobalt id

Metro Books
122 Fifth Avenue
New York, NY 10011

ISBN-13: 978-0-7607-8164-7
ISBN-10: 0-7607-8164-8

Typeset in Times NR MT
Colour reproduction by Scanhouse, Malaysia
Printed and bound by Imago, Thailand

10 9 8 7 6 5 4 3

Contents

Introduction

Some of the most familiar things around us once had deeper and more fascinating meanings and associations than we now realize. They made up a language of traditional symbols used by artists and craftsmen to convey ideas about human life and about both the natural and supernatural worlds. Like signs, symbols form a kind of visual shorthand, but one with more emotional, psychological and spiritual resonance. Symbolism is the emotional or spiritual heightening of an object, graphic form or ritual action that may be simple in itself.

Symbols predate writing as a way of communicating large ideas. Carved, painted or worked into effigies, clothing or ornaments, they were used for magical purposes, to ward off evil or to entreat or placate gods – and also to control societies, to weld them together, inspiring loyalty, obedience, aggression, love or fear. A coherent system of dynamic symbols could make people feel in harmony with themselves, their community and the cosmos. It could also inspire collective action. People still fight and die under emblems, banners or flags that have symbolic significance.

Many fundamental ideas, and the symbols for them, have appeared in various different societies, ranging from primitive cultures to the developed civilizations of Asia, India, the Middle East, Europe and Central America. The near-universal occurrence of certain forms led the Swiss psychotherapist Carl Jung to believe that symbols or "archetypes" are deeply embedded in the human psyche and that we respond to them instinctively.

Features of the earth or the visible universe – animals, plants, stars and stones – are all included in the symbolic repertoire. These were once seen as reflections of a greater reality, having qualities expressive of laws and moral "truths" inherent in the cosmic order. But not all symbols are iconic. Graphic images are symbols when they stand for an idea or abstract quality, and ritual actions can symbolize a shared emotional or spiritual experience.

The spiritual and physical quest of alchemy was represented in symbolic terms by its medieval practitioners. Here the King and Queen symbolize the male (solar) and female (lunar) principles which must be united as part of the quest.

Although the advance of science has drained ancient symbols of their imaginative force, symbolism constantly renews itself as a way of giving significance to human life. Traditional symbols reappear in new forms – disastrously so in the case of the swastika, which originally had positive meaning. Others, like the white dove of peace, continue as a force for good. Symbolism, like music and art, speaks to emotional and spiritual needs that the language of reason can never fully express.

The Spirit Incarnate

For millennia, humans have viewed themselves not as finite assemblages of matter but as mortal vessels filled with a timeless spiritual essence. The body and the processes of birth, life and death were given symbolic meanings that expressed this larger dimension.

In many cultures, divinities were shaped after the human form – often with additional heads or limbs to convey their superior powers. The gods could be incarnated and human beings could use shamanic magic to transcend their bodies and achieve oneness with the spiritual dimension. So strong was the sense of a unifying divine wholeness that the original state of being was seen as androgynous, not only in Mesoamerican, Greek, Aboriginal and Egyptian mythology but also in Platonic philosophy and Sufi mysticism. Just as the Indian god Shiva contained a female side, Parvati, so the implication of the Book of Genesis is that Adam contained Eve. Male and female were seen as aspects of one nature – divine and human – a complementary unity summed up by the Chinese yin–yang symbol shown below.

Shiva, depicted right with multiple arms and weapons symbolizing his powers, is one of the most protean of the Indian gods, sometimes destructive, at other times a benign herdsman of souls. The various forms he takes, together with his fickle behaviour, suggest an attempt to personify the bewildering diversity of human nature itself.

Creation

The dominant symbol for the mystery of original creation is the **EGG**. Few simple natural objects have such self-explanatory yet profound meaning. For early myth-makers, the image of a god bursting fully-formed from the shell of an egg captured in microcosm the miracle of life arising from the primordial void. The egg is thus an emblem of potentiality; once shattered, it releases the complementary forces necessary to the dynamics of creation. These forces are often symbolized by the division of a bisexual god or by the breaking apart of male and female gods, as in the Maori myth of how Rangi formed the sky by tearing himself from the arms of his wife Papa, the earth. Alternatively, the forces may be elemental, as in the Nordic creative conflict of fire and ice. In Chinese myth, the cosmic giant and divine ancestor Pan Gu grew for 18,000 years inside a cosmic egg until it split into two parts, a light half (the heavens) and a dark half (the earth).

This mythical Polynesian "birdman", painted on an Easter Island rock, holds an egg, believed to symbolize the origin of the cosmos and of all living things.

The **WATERS** on which the primeval egg floats are themselves a widespread creation symbol – formless, limitless, inexhaustible and full of possibilities. In Genesis, God moves upon the face of these primordial waters. In Indian mythology, the Hindu creator-god Vishnu sleeps on a serpent coiled upon the sea. According to Egypt's creation mythology, the first form to arise from the primeval watery chaos (Nun) was a mound providing a perch for the Benu bird, personifying the creator sun god. In Mesopotamian myth, life arose from the mingling of Apsu, the sweet waters on which the earth floated, and the salt waters personified by Tiamat, the chaos goddess whose destruction led to the evolution of an organized world.

The theme of destruction as a primal stage in the process of creation is common to many cosmogonies in which a cosmic god dies or a race of Titans or **GIANTS** is vanquished. In Norse myth, the primeval giant Ymir is dismembered, his body, blood and skull becoming earth, sea and

Celtic fertility rites in which victims were crammed into a colossal "wicker man" and burned may derive from ancient ideas that the sacrifice of primeval giants was necessary to the process of creation.

sky. In psychology, giants are seen as emblems of parental authority (hence their exaggerated size), leading to the suggestion that their creation-destruction symbolism has a Freudian basis. In a wider sense, ancient legends of the defeat of giants can be seen as allegories of the struggle for social evolution against primitive barbarian forces or against the elemental forces of the earth.

The organization of matter through the imposition of order over formless mass is an essential aspect of creation mythology. Four geometric designs in Egyptian hieroglyphics express this process – a spiral symbolizing divine energy, a spiral in a square symbolizing energy at work in the cosmos, a cloudy shape representing undifferentiated matter, and a square alone, symbol of the ordered world.

THE EGG IN MYTH AND FOLKLORE

In folklore throughout the world, the egg is a propitious symbol, suggesting luck, wealth and health. Magical eggs of gold or silver are guarded by dragons; and from eggs gods and heroes are born. In one story, Helen of Troy came from an egg that had fallen from the moon. Alternatively she was born from an egg laid by Leda, queen of Sparta, after she had coupled with a swan (the god Zeus in disguise). Later that night Leda also slept with her mortal husband. She laid two eggs; from one came Polydeuces and Helen, and from the other Castor and Clytemnestra.

Also associated with the promise and hope of spring, the egg took a ready-made place in Christian Easter ceremonies as a symbol of resurrection. Eucharistic implications are suggested by the tradition of eating eggs at the end of Lent. In Jewish custom, at the Seder meal the egg is a symbol of promise, and traditionally it is the first food offered to Jewish mourners.

A Ukranian painted egg depicts reindeer standing beneath the Tree of Life. These motifs, like the egg itself, are widespread, appearing as benevolent symbols of creativity and regeneration in both North American and European art.

A curious old folkloric notion that **OSTRICH EGGS** hatch themselves is connected to the use in art of an egg to symbolize the Immaculate Conception – as in Piero della Francesca's altarpiece *Madonna and Child* (*c.*1450); ostrich eggs also feature as symbols of resurrection on tombs found in Coptic churches.

In many myths, ranging from Egypt and India to the Far East and Oceania, the initial process of creation and birth begins when a **COSMIC EGG** (sometimes fertilized by a serpent but more often laid in the primeval sea by a giant bird) gives form to chaos, and from it hatches the sun (the golden yolk), leading to the division of earth and sky, and the multiplicity of life, natural and supernatural.

The creation symbolism of the egg is strengthened by the egg shape of the testicles and by the sexual duality of the egg's yolk and white: in the Congo, the yolk stands for female warmth, while the white symbolizes male sperm.

The Female Principle

Paleolithic carvings, perhaps 30,000 years old, suggest that the earliest of all fertility symbols may have been the **MOTHER**. And although many cosmogonies identify male or dual-sex creator divinities as the original source of life, it is possible that they were predated by worship of maternal goddesses personifying nature, the earth or the creative force itself. Hesiod (*c.*700BC), the poet who first systematized Greek mythology, placed Ge or Gaia (the earth) first in his genealogy of the gods as the "universal mother, firmly founded, the oldest of divinities". She bore the gods and, according to Attic myth, the first human, Erichthonius. In the Greco-Roman world, worship of maternal nature symbols including Rhea and Demeter culminated in the cult of the Phrygian Great Mother, Cybele, an early rival to Christianity.

The Christian cult of the Virgin Mary is unique because she represented a complete break with a long tradition of venerated mothers who were essentially nature symbols. Her symbolic link with earlier mother goddesses is that her son was killed. The death, emasculation or dismemberment of the mother goddess's loved ones is a great recurring theme in the mythic symbolism of the mother – representing the death-rebirth cycle that is the iron rule of nature.

Isis, the great Egyptian goddess, wears a headdress symbolizing the traditional role of women as nourishers of life. Her crescent horns combine the female lunar and cow fertility symbolism; they cradle the male solar disk in an image that proclaims divine unity.

Kali, the "Dark Mother" of Hindu mythology, is the most alarming image of the female as creator-destroyer. Multiple aspects of the divine female were sometimes represented in iconography by triform or triple goddesses, as with Hecate and in Celtic carvings. Multiple breasts identified fertility goddesses. Celtic mother goddesses were usually protective, especially of animals, including wild beasts. In art, mother attributes include boats or rudders, as well as familiar emblems of fertility and prosperity such as baskets of fruit, sheaves of corn or cornucopias.

Female emblems such as fountains, lakes, oceans, rivers and the moon, especially its crescent form, together with containers such as baskets and cups all continue the dominant ancient symbolism of **WOMAN** as receptor, carrier, animator, protector and nourisher of life.

The symbolic archetype of womanhood was the **QUEEN** often depicted in art and literature as a personification of the moon. She was linked with the king (see page 15) in a duality seen as necessary for the prosperity and happiness of the realm. In alchemy, the sacred marriage of the white queen (mercury) and red king (sulphur) symbolized the union of male and female principles to produce the Philosopher's Stone.

GENITAL SYMBOLISM IN ART

The female principle is graphically represented in iconography most directly by the **LOZENGE**. A symbol of the life matrix, the vulva, fertility and, in some contexts, innocence, it takes on dual imagery when combined with the phallic symbolism of snakes in Native American decorative art. Lozenge shapes appear with fertility symbolism on the jade skirt of the Mexican goddess of rivers and lakes, Chalchiuhtlicue, consort of the god Tlaloc. In Mali, a half-lozenge shape with a point at the other end was a symbol for a young woman.

In Christian art, the lozenge emblem of pagan fertility goddesses was taken over and spiritualized as a virginity symbol. The Virgin Mary is conventionally shown within a **MANDORLA**, an almond-shaped aureole that signifies purity and virginity. As the **YONI**, the vulva is an important motif in Tantric Buddhist art, depicted as two adjoining arcs symbolizing the gateway to spiritual rebirth. It symbolizes the Tantric view of the world's existence as a continuous birthing process, and is paralleled by the notion of continuous ecstatic fertilization thorough the male organ, represented by the lingam. In Hinduism, the yoni can appear as a ring or rings at the base of the lingam dedicated to Shiva as creator.

A less direct symbol of the vulva, widely popular in art, is the **SHELL**, an auspicious, erotic, lunar and feminine emblem linked with conception, regeneration, baptism and, in many traditions, prosperity – probably through its association with fecundity.

In Botticelli's famous painting, the foam-born love goddess, Venus, shields her vulva, which is nevertheless depicted in the symbolic form of the shell that carries her to shore.

The Male Principle

Supreme gods of mythology and religion are usually, but not always, personified as father figures – not surprisingly, given the patriarchal nature of most traditional cultures. Reflecting this dominance, the **FATHER** is symbolically associated with solar and sky power, spiritual, moral and civil authority, reason and consciousness, law, the elements of air and fire, warlike spirit, and the thunderbolt. More specific male symbols include the sun, fire and lightning, and a host of vertical or penetrative objects, such as the arrow, cone, lance, lingam, obelisk, pillar, or pole, plough, rod, spade, spear, sword, thunderbolt and torch.

The **PHALLUS** itself is a solar and active fertility symbol widely believed to be lucky and protective. The overscale erect phalluses sometimes depicted in art usually have symbolic rather than erotic significance. Figures of Priapus, the hideous but enormously well-endowed son of the god Dionysus (Bacchus, in Roman myth) and goddess Aphrodite (Venus) were placed in Greek and Roman gardens, vineyards and orchards; his phallus, often painted red, was believed to encourage growth and scare away both thieves and crows. Ancient phallic funerary objects symbolize the continuity of life after death. Phallic-shaped talismans were popular

The ancient notion of kings as symbols of prosperity and delegates of the sun was still alive in 18th-century France when Louis XVI was executed as hostage to France's declining fortunes.

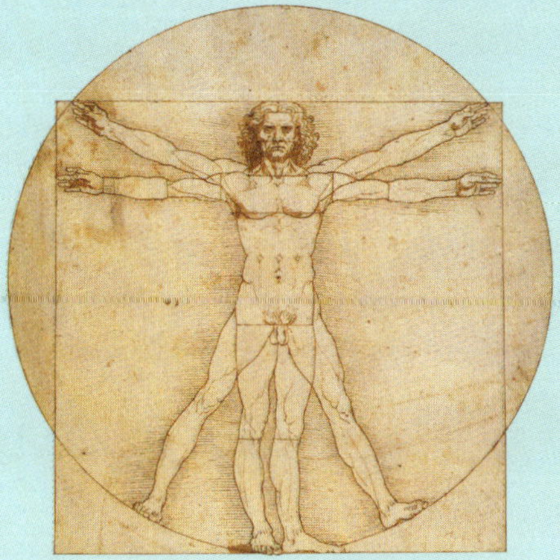

A mystic belief in man as the paragon of animals underlies Leonardo's depiction of a male figure as a pentagram formed by arms, legs and head, representing the universe in microcosm.

with farmers and fishermen, and were also used as charms against sterility.

Phallic symbolism famously survives in European folkloric traditions of the **MAYPOLE**. A spring emblem of fertility and solar renewal, it is linked to ancient agricultural and resurrection rites and also to the axial symbolism of the World Tree. In England, the phallic symbolism of maypoles and wanton behaviour around them on May Day affronted the Puritans. Pagan sources of the maypole include the Greek and Roman spring rites of Attis, slain consort of the Earth Mother, Cybele. His symbol was a stripped pine tree, wound with woollen bands, around which dances were performed to invoke and celebrate his resurrection. The Roman festival of Hilaria adapted this tradition, combined with other, existing spring rites as it spread into the Celtic world.

An important role in male symbolism is played by the **BEARD**, which represented dignity, sovereignty, virility and wisdom. Male divinities are commonly bearded in iconography, and in Egypt beardless rulers – including queens – were shown with false beards as a mark of status.

The symbolic male archetype is the **KING**, representing divinely sanctioned power and absolute temporal authority over a tribe or nation. The stronger the king's symbolic link with supernatural forces, the more crucial became his leadership qualities, intelligence and health – authority going hand in hand with responsibility for the happiness of his subjects, hence the ancient sacrifices of the king (or his representative) when countries were overtaken by plagues or crop failures.

THE PHALLUS IN HINDU TRADITION

In the cave of Elephanta at Bombay, the **LINGAM** – a thick, smooth cone of black stone – was the focus of circumambulation rituals, indicating its role as an axial symbol as well as a phallic one, somewhat like the classical omphalos (the "navel of the world"). In one myth, Shiva's lingam appears as a pillar of light, the upper and lower limits of which cannot be found by Brahma as a wild goose or Vishnu as a boar – proof of Shiva's power. Essentially a virility symbol, the lingam may appear with a circle at its base representing the yoni (vulva).

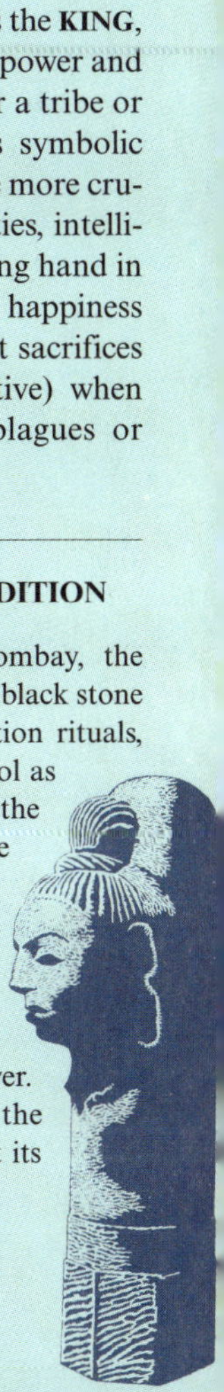

The male generative force in nature is symbolized in Hindu art by a stylized lingam (phallus) representing the god Shiva as divine procreator.

The Body

In most symbolic traditions, idealizations of **NAKEDNESS** represent innocence, freedom, vulnerability, truth and, often, divinity. Although nakedness can also symbolize carnality, shame or wickedness, the unadorned body was frequently a symbol of purity. Hence the disrobing of initiates and priests in some ancient religious rites. Ascetics have sometimes gone naked for the same reason, and modern witch covens use nakedness to symbolize their openness to supernatural forces.

A richly complex symbolism is attached to many individual parts of the body. The **MOUTH**, for example, is often shown open in iconography – sometimes as a devouring symbol, sometimes to indicate that spirits are speaking. In Egyptian funerary rites, the mouths of the dead were opened to enable their *ka* (creative energy) to give evidence in the judgment hall of the afterlife and to receive the gift of new life. Solar disks were placed in the mouths of the dead, as were jade objects (symbolizing immortality) in China and Mexico. Jung saw a symbolic link between the mouth – as red and consuming – and fire, expressed in fire-breathing dragon legends.

The **TEETH** are primordial emblems of aggressive-defensive power, which explains why shamans wear necklaces of animal teeth; conversely, drawing or loss of teeth is a symbol of castration or impotence .

The **NAVEL** has widespread symbolism as the source of life and is often exaggerated in African statuary for this reason. It is also seen as a centre of creative and psychic energy, a focus of yogic concentration. In Vedic tradition, the lotus of creation grew from the navel of Vishnu as he rested on the cosmic waters, giving birth to Brahma.

The Bible's account of Adam and Eve's expulsion from Eden associates their nakedness with the primal state of innocence before the Fall. Their concealing hands in Masaccio's painting conveys their loss of this natural state of grace.

The **BELLY** was seen as the seat of life in Oriental tradition, hence the significance in Japan of ritual disembowelment, *harakiri*, and the use of a fat belly to symbolize prosperity. There are many ancient links between the **INTESTINES** and magical knowledge, which lie behind the expression "having a gut feeling". The Egyptians kept intestines of eviscerated corpses in urns, as repositories of the powers needed by the soul on its journey to the afterworld; and examining entrails to divine the future was an Etruscan and Roman pseudoscience.

Images of **FEET** sometimes appear in iconography to indicate contact between the earth and a divinity. In Buddhism, for example, the immanence of the Buddha is symbolized by the soles of his feet, which bear seven symbols of divine wisdom: conch, crown, diamond sceptre, fish, vase, swastika and Wheel of the Law.

Going barefoot, as in some mendicant orders, signifies humility. Christ's washing of his disciple's feet was a gesture that was imitated by English sovereigns who washed the feet of the poor to show their humility.

THE TONGUE IN AGGRESSIVE DISPLAY

Often shown protruding in carvings and paintings, the **TONGUE** is a forceful aggressive-defensive symbol because it is the only organ of the body that can be so startlingly displayed. The **EXTENDED TONGUE** in Maori art and *hakas* (war dances) expresses challenge and defiance (as does everyday tongue-poking), and it is also a common sexual symbol in primitive art, such as fertility "pole figures" from Borneo. The protective god Bes in Egypt appears with a protruding tongue, which is believed to ward off evil. There is a strong symbolic link between tongues and flames – both are red, active, consuming and creative-destructive – thus the Indian fire god Agni is shown with seven tongues. The tongue can also symbolize language, eloquence or wisdom; in Egyptian funerary art, extended tongues allowed the dead to speak to the gods. Some animal effigies with protruding tongues invoke rain.

Displayed tongues often have a demonic or carnivorous symbolism. In India, the goddess Kali's tongue symbolizes her consuming power.

Hair

Hair is a deeply significant aspect of the human body both socially and personally, as can be seen from the wide range of symbolism attached to different hair styles. Essentially, it is associated with the life force.

The power symbolism of hair growth is exemplified by Samson, a warrior of the ancient Hebrew Nazarite sect whose **LONG HAIR** was a sign of charismatic holiness and physical strength. The Khalsa community of Sikhs let their hair and beards grow for similar reasons. In many societies long hair was a mark of royal power or of liberty and independence, as among the Gauls and other Celtic peoples. Long, loose hair in women signified the unmarried state, or virginity – as in Christian iconography of the Virgin Mary and virgin saints – compared with the braided hair of the courtesan. Alternatively, as in Russia, a single braid marked the maiden, double braids the wife. Letting down bound hair was a permissive sexual signal.

The Buddha often appears with a shaven head, symbolizing the renunciation of vanities. But in this Korean statue, stylized, close-cropped curled hair symbolizes control and composure.

Whereas body hair was associated mainly with virility or lower states of being (hairiness is a devilish attribute in Christian art), head hair was intimately linked with the individual spirit or vital force of a person – an idea that accounts for the custom of keeping **LOCKS OF HAIR**. In ancient Greece, taking a lock of hair from a dead person released his soul into the underworld. Scalping, in Native American warfare, removed an enemy's power; braves daringly left a lock of hair on their shaven heads to goad their foe. Islamic custom was to leave a tuft by which the faithful could be drawn upward into paradise.

Although hermits traditionally let their hair grow, many religious orders have followed the priestly Egyptian custom of shaving the hair as a symbol of submission to God or renunciation of the material world. Submission (to the Manchus) was also the original symbolism of the Chinese **PIGTAIL**. **CUTTING HAIR** was close to a castration symbol in ancient China – and remains a resented symbol of conformity to military discipline in some countries.

HAIR COLOUR has its own symbolism, red hair once having demonic associations, golden hair standing for solar or kingly power, and black for terrestrial authority. Dishevelled hair can symbolize asceticism – an attribute of the Hindu god Shiva who appears with wild locks.

The Gorgon Medusa, with her hair of writhing snakes, is a symbol of the female life force in its malevolent and destructive aspect.

Right: Christian symbolism is at full flow in this touchingly vulnerable portrait of Mary Magdalene by Giotto. Her unloosed tresses not only depict the saint who washed Christ's feet with her hair but also proclaim her chastity.

Heart, Blood and Head

The **HEART** is the symbolic source of the affections – love, compassion, charity, joy or sorrow – but also of spiritual illumination, truth and intelligence. It was often equated with the soul. Symbolically, the heart was the body's sun, animating all. Ritual application of this belief led the Aztecs to sacrifice thousands of victims and offer their hearts to the sun each year to sustain its power. As a symbol of what is most essential in a human being, the heart was left in the eviscerated bodies of Egyptian mummies.

St Augustine holds a flaming heart in Tiepolo's painting of the education of Louis IX of France, who was himself canonized in 1297.

The heart is an emblem of truth, conscience or moral courage in many religions – the temple or throne of God in Islamic and Judeo-Christian thought; the divine centre, or atman, and the Third Eye of transcendent wisdom in Hinduism; the diamond of purity and essence of the Buddha; the Taoist centre of understanding. The "Sacred Heart" of Christ became a focus of Roman Catholic worship as a symbol of the Lord's redeeming love, sometimes shown pierced by nails and with a crown of thorns, in reference to the Crucifixion. A **FLAMING HEART** is the attribute of SS Augustine and Antony of Padua. A heart on fire is a key symbol of the ardent Christian but also an attribute in art of Charity and of profane passion – as in Renaissance paintings of the Greek goddess Aphrodite (in Roman myth, Venus). The **HEART TRANSFIXED** by Eros's (Cupid's) arrow was another Renaissance theme, which became the motif of St Valentine's Day – a mid-February festival with pagan rather than Christian roots.

In iconography, the heart takes on a vase-like shape, symbolizing something into which love is poured or carried; in this sense it is linked with the Holy Grail.

An ancient Egyptian papyrus depicts a heart being weighed against a "truth feather" in the underworld to see if it is heavy with misdeeds, or light enough to pass on to paradise.

BLOOD is itself a ritual symbol of life force, believed in many cultures to contain a share of divine energy or, more commonly, the spirit of an individual creature. Blood

had rain-bearing or fertilizing power according to some ancient traditions, as in Middle-Eastern marriage ceremonies where the bride stepped over the sprinkled blood of a sheep. Bull's blood was used for its supposed magical power in the Roman rites of Mithras and Cybele. In the Roman *taurobolium*, initiates were led into a pit to be drenched by the blood of bull sacrifices. The mingling of blood is a symbol of union in many folk customs (as for example in blood brotherhood) and can mark a seal or covenant between men or between humans and God. In Roman Catholic doctrine, Christ is present in the transubstantiated wine of the Eucharist, embodying as well as symbolizing the Saviour's blood.

THE POWER SYMBOLISM OF THE HEAD

The ancient value placed upon the **SEVERED HEAD** of an enemy was based less on its role as the instrument of reason and thought than on the idea that it contained the person's spirit, power or life force. In many traditions the head replaces the heart as the presumed location of the soul. For many peoples, including Celtic warriors who wore heads as trophies, the head had fertility or phallic symbolism and was thought to transmit the strength and courage of the decapitated warrior to its new owner. In iconography, the head of a god, king or hero, mounted on a pillar, shown on a coin, or used as a funerary emblem, embodied his or her power to influence events. For Plato, the sphere of the head represented a human microcosm.

In hybrid animal-gods, the head may indicate which part of the creature has dominance. Artists could increase the force of an image by multiplying heads or faces, sometimes to indicate different functions. Thus in Roman iconography, three-headed Hecate moved between heaven, earth and the underworld. The four heads of Brahma refer to the four Hindu Vedas, the four ram heads of Amun-Ra to his rulership of all the elements.

In art, heads of the Greek twins Castor and Polydeuces shown with one looking up and one down symbolized ascending and descending phases of heavenly bodies. Images combining male and female heads had protective symbolism in Egypt. Headdresses and head movements – bowed in submission, raised in pride – have particular significance in human gesture.

A pre-Toltec Guatemalan stele shows a priest severing the head of a victim in a solar worship sacrifice. The head could take the place of a ball used in cult games as an emblem of the sun. Falling serpents symbolize streaming blood.

Hand and Eye

The executive role of the **HAND** in human life and the belief that it can transmit spiritual as well as physical energy has made it a symbol of power (spiritual and temporal), action, strength and protection. It was sometimes an image forceful enough to stand alone in iconography, as a motif in cave paintings, for example, or in Christian paintings of God's hand appearing from the clouds. Belief that the hands of kings, religious leaders or miracle workers had beneficial power existed from ancient times; hence the laying-on of hands in healing or in religious blessing, confirmation and ordination. Talismanic use of the hands extended to the grisly practice of thieves, carrying the severed right hand of a hanged criminal for nefarious good luck.

The Egyptian wedjat symbolizes cosmic wholeness and the all-seeing power of the sky god Horus.

Western and most other traditions probably assign more symbolic value to the **RIGHT** than to the **LEFT** for no better reason than that most people are right-handed. With few exceptions, the right is associated with precedence, action and the solar, male principle, the left with secondary position, weakness, passivity and the lunar, female principle. In China the concept of yin–yang harmony made for a less rigid division of symbolic values. If anything, the left is usually given precedence, as in Japan: it is associated with honour, nobility, wisdom and the male, celestial and solar principle, while the right is limited with lunar and female qualities.

Although the conceptual link between hand and power (words synonymous in ancient Hebrew) is overwhelmingly important in pictorial symbolism, it is only one aspect of the much more extensive and varied symbolism of hand gestures. These form in Hindu and Buddhist mudras an

In Christian symbolism, the raised hand signifies blessing or benediction. This painting of Christ as saviour shows him with two fingers open, symbolizing teaching and judgment.

entire symbolic language involving hundreds of hand and finger shapes and positions deployed in religious ritual, dance and theatre. In iconography, an eye in a palm is a symbol of clairvoyance or, in Buddhism, of compassionate wisdom.

For Muslims, the open hand of Fatima (daughter of Muhammad) represents both the hand of God and the five fundamentals of Islam: faith, prayer, pilgrimage, fasting and charity.

The **EYE** is visually an even more compelling symbol than the hand. In Western symbolism, the right eye is active and solar; the left passive and lunar (a system reversed in Eastern tradition). Egyptian myth held that the lunar eye of the sky god Horus had been restored after its destruction in a battle with Set – the god of disorder and sterility – a story that accounts for the popularity of the wedjat eye symbol as a protective device on amulets. Eyes were also painted or carved on Egyptian tombs to protect the dead in the afterworld. Winged eyes in Egyptian iconography represent north and south.

The occult **THIRD EYE**, sometimes called the "eye of the heart", symbolizes the eye of spiritual perception, associated with the power of Shiva and the synthesizing element of fire in Hinduism, with inner vision in Buddhism, and with clairvoyance in the Islamic faith. Although an eye is depicted on the forehead of Shiva, it is an inner eye. Its antithesis is the **EVIL EYE** which, in Islamic tradition, is a symbol of the destructive force of envy. The Gorgon Medusa, whose gaze could turn men to stone, was an earlier, Greek symbol of the evil eye. Perseus used a mirror to aim the blow that killed her, and eye talismans serve a similar deflecting function. In medieval Europe, the horseshoe was thought to be particularly effective against the evil eye of witchcraft or Satan himself, sometimes depicted with a displaced eye on his body.

MULTIPLE EYES had positive symbolism in some traditions, representing vigilance and the light of stars in the sky. The peacock attribute of Amitabha, the Tibetan Buddha of Infinite Light, has this symbolism (through multi-eyed plumage).

Eyes of other animals had clairvoyant meaning. Hence the Parsee custom of bringing a dog to a deathbed so that the dying could see the afterworld in its eyes, and the belief of Aztec shamans that they could see the spirit world in a jaguar's eyes.

The solar eye symbolizes the omniscience of sky gods. A single eye also appears as a symbol of God in early Christian art.

The Mortal Span

The brevity of human life, the fear of death, and the hope of rebirth were all major symbolic themes in the philosophy, mythology and religion of ancient cultures. The passage from one stage of life to the next was marked both by ritual and by personifications such as **FATHER TIME** with his scythe, or the **CHILD**, often depicted in a paradisal landscape, free of anxiety – an emblem of purity, potentiality, innocence and spontaneity. The theme of lost youth appears in many legends of rejuvenating springs. Dating back at least to Roman times is the popular Western notion of a **FOUNTAIN OF YOUTH**. In art, Cupid conventionally presides over this fountain, its jetting waters symbolizing the sexual life force and proclaiming the rejuvenating effects of falling in love.

This shamanic creature, part-human, part-animal, is from the late Paleolithic period (c.10,000BC). A Dordogne cave image, it may be an emblem of regeneration, a common symbolism of antlers.

LONGEVITY is a preoccupation in the symbol system of China. Its most common emblems are trees or their fruits, notably the apple, bamboo, cedar, citron, cypress, myrtle, oak, palm, peach, pear, pine and plum. The colour green and stones such as jade, diamond and ruby, and rock itself, also represent longevity, together with a host of animals such as the crane, dove, elephant, hare, phoenix, stork, toad, and turtle.

Death (as a woman) dances with the Devil in a Mexican wood carving. Skeletons dancing with Death are used to symbolize the ephemerality of carnal pleasures.

The Indian philosophies of Hinduism and Buddhism are not alone in reminding mortals that attachment to the material body and its pleasures is vain. In Western art, vanity is a major field for symbolism. Countless still-life paintings show material possessions such as coins, gold or jewels, and trappings of power such as crowns or sceptres, together with images of emptiness like overturned cups or *memento mori*, particularly the **SKULL** – all symbols intended to remind viewers of the evanescence of life and the folly of clinging to the things of this world.

In Hindu iconography, a skull filled with blood symbolizes the need to freely renounce life. The **WHEEL**, turning through endless cycles of creation, existence and destruction, was a powerful Hindu and Buddhist emblem of the disadvantages of reincarnation. In most earlier societies, the skull and other elements of the **SKELETON** had more positive symbolism as the parts of the body most resistant to decay and likeliest to form a basis for bodily resurrection. Bones were carefully protected in many ancient cultures for this reason, often under megaliths. Northern European peoples from Finland to Siberia buried the skeletons of bears and other game to ensure their rebirth. In one Scandinavian myth, Thor uses the bones of goats to bring them back to life after feasting on their flesh. When he notices one of them limping, he is furious with the son of his host because he deduces that the boy has sucked the marrow from its leg bone. The concept of things bred or felt "in the bone" echoes ancient beliefs that the essence of a person – in Mali, the soul itself – was contained in the bone.

DEATH AND ITS EMBLEMS

Personifications of death as an absolute are usually alarming. Religious symbolism modifies the image of finality, suggesting that death is a necessary stage which results in liberation to immortality. The symbolism of fear and hope sometimes appear side by side in uneasy combination. In art, the most familiar figure of Death is the **SKELETAL RIDER**, cloaked and cowled, pitilessly wielding a scythe, trident, sword or bow and arrows. He holds an hourglass signifying the measured span of life. Underworld gods who ruled over the dead used such grim auxiliaries to despatch souls to them but were not themselves necessarily frightening symbols. The Druids taught that the god of death (Donn in Ireland) was the source of all life. Other symbols of death include the skeleton, the skull, the tomb, or a black-cloaked figure with a sword, such as the Greek god Thanatos (black is associated with death in Occidental tradition, white in Oriental). Death could also appear as a drummer or dancer. Gentler symbols were a veiled woman or an Angel of Death, such as the Islamic Israfil. Death ships or barges symbolized the journey to the afterworld. Among plants, the poppy, asphodel and cypress are common death symbols.

Details in Pieter Bruegel's The Triumph of Death *reflect religious persecutions in the Netherlands during the 1560s. Death preoccupied artists as first plague, then war, swept across Europe.*

Soul, Mind and the Supernatural

Symbolism seeks to give form to the intangible. Nowhere is this more true than in magic, ritual and religion – the attempts of different societies to communicate with the supernatural forces presumed to lie behind the visible world. The history of symbolism shows a slow movement away from the idea that humans are collectively at the mercy of fickle gods. As societies have become more sophisticated, artists and religious symbolists have increasingly dramatized human choice in a dualistic universe of light and dark, good and evil, salvation and damnation, virtue and vice. This view of the world as a battleground with every principle set against its opposite was based on observation of dichotomies both in the natural world and in human nature itself. This can be seen at its simplest level in the recurrent symbolism of twins, one good, the other evil, as in Iroquois myths. Set against it was the hope of a spiritual equilibrium, symbolized in the alchemical image of the sun and moon below.

William Blake's image of the Archangel Michael binding Satan and casting him down shows the symbolic power of the idea that two antagonistic forces are at work in the world and are irreconcilable. Yet many symbolic traditions depict no struggle between good and evil. To the Taoist, evil is simply disorder.

Heaven and Hell

Belief in the **AFTERLIFE** has created some of the richest of all symbol systems. Egyptian and Tibetan Books of the Dead lay down precise rules for conduct during and after death, and Chinese, Japanese, Mesoamerican, Buddhist, Muslim, Hindu and Christian eschatological texts similarly give guidance, but in less elaborate form.

In relatively primitive societies, the afterworld was often imagined to be a happier version of the world as we know it. In the distinct afterworlds of monotheistic religions, the symbolism of bliss or misery is remarkably consistent: paradise lies above the vault of the sky (architecturally symbolized by the dome and stupa), sparkling with light and harmonious with music; hell lies below – dark, smoky, putrid and painful or, less often, desolately frozen.

Most traditions envisaged a **SOUL** inhabiting the body, sometimes wandering from it during dreams and persisting in some form after death. In Egypt the soul that left the body was symbolized by a human-headed hawk, the Ba, while in Western art, souls often appear as naked children. Semitic and other mystic traditions envisage the soul as a spark – a fragment of divine light separated from the Godhead in the dualistic universe of light and darkness but able to rejoin it once freed from the material world.

Butterflies as symbols of the soul and resurrection are found as far apart as Congo, Mexico and Polynesia. They also appear on Christian tombs.

The kind of **PARADISE** depicted by artists often represented only a transitional stage toward something ineffable, symbolized by pure light. Heaven was constructed in a series of layers or spheres (thus the Islamic Seventh Heaven in which Muhammad reached the Throne of Allah). From celestial cities or gardens the righteous soul ascended toward an abstract bliss, the contemplation of God's radiance. This level of transcendence corresponds in

The divide between life and death was often symbolized by a river, as in Joachim Patenier's picture of the Greek Styx, with its ferryman, Chiron. Or it might involve a sea journey, as in Oceanic tradition.

Hindu and Buddhist thought to nirvana – a state in which the individual is finally released from cyclic reincarnation, extinguished as "self" but absorbed into the ultimate reality. Although such pure illumination lies beyond objective description, its clarity has been likened in Buddhism to the brilliance of the full moon revealed by parting clouds.

IMMORTALITY is widely symbolized by the butterfly, which provides a perfect analogy of life (the crawling caterpillar), death (the dark chrysalis) and rebirth (the soul fluttering free). Hence the depictions of Christ holding the butterfly of resurrection and use of the butterfly in Aztec culture to represent the souls of slain warriors.

One of the most widespread symbols of a non-celestial heaven is the **ISLAND**. Symbolically, it is always a magical "elsewhere", a world set apart. The island may be a spiritual goal or centre reserved for elected immortals (such as the Happy Isles of classical mythology and the mystic Islands of the Blessed in China), or an enchanted place like Prospero's island in Shakespeare's *The Tempest* where wrongs are righted.

For a number of cultures, **HEAVEN** was the province of the elite – the Scandinavian Valhalla, for example, was the destination of heroes fallen in battle and the Elysian fields of Greek myth were reserved for the fortunate few. In other traditions, heaven is attainable by those who use the correct rituals or spells in the underworld (as in ancient Egypt) or those who expiate minor sins in an afterworld such as the Catholic Purgatory. **HELL** is not necessarily final either, although medieval Christianity relished the concept of eternal hellfire.

Scales symbolize divine judgment in this Christian picture of the archangel Michael. Each pan of the scales holds a tiny human figure; a demon slyly tips the scales.

RETRIBUTION is a common theme, sometimes symbolized by the weighing of souls. Judgment for Tibetan Buddhists was weighed out in black and white pebbles; for Japanese Buddhists by reference to red and white severed heads. Other trials involved dangerous journeys – perhaps a bridge to be crossed, which would prove narrow and slippery for sinners but broad and stable for the virtuous.

Good and Evil

The concept of good and evil as inherent contending forces in the cosmos is largely an invention of the great Persian magus, Zoroaster (Zarathustra) *c.*628–551BC. He built upon older symbolic traditions in which **LIGHT** was a metaphor for divinity, signifying the presence of a cosmic power of ultimate goodness and truth. Although most philosophical traditions recognize light and **DARKNESS** as a necessary duality, the monotheistic religions of the Near East, Judaism, Christianity and Islam followed Zoroaster in seeing them as ethically opposed kingdoms of good and evil.

Divine will is symbolized by the anthropomorphic winged forms called **ANGELS**. Thought to be evolved from Semitic and Egyptian winged deities, angels appear in a number of religions, but their symbolism is most elaborate in the Islamic, Jewish and Christian faiths. Attributes in art include trumpets, harps, swords, censers and sceptres or wands. Angels appear variously in the roles of messengers (Greek *angeloi*), warriors and guardians or protectors. **ARCHANGELS** have specific and personalized symbolism. In art, Gabriel, as divine herald of the Annunciation, holds a lily or sceptre with fleur de lis; Michael, as warrior-guardian of the Righteous and instrument of judgment, holds a sword or scales; and Raphael, as protector of children and travellers, holds a staff.

Darkness is, like the colour black, an ambivalent symbol standing not only for death, sin, ignorance and evil but also for potential life – the darkness of germination. Thus it has negative meanings only when considered within the duality of light and dark. In the ancient world – and generally in Asia, Africa, Oceania and North America, evil was seen more as an occasional than as an inherent tendency in nature. Often equated with misfortune, it was symbolized by monsters, goblins or by dual-nature divinities with capricious and destructive as well as benevolent aspects.

Radiance flooding behind the figure in William Blake's Glad Day *draws on the ancient symbolism of light as the embodiment of divine goodness.*

Humbaba (sculpted 4,000 years ago) was one of a host of Babylonian demons thought to account for misfortunes.

The idea of the **DEVIL** is derived from Zoroaster who proposed the existence of such a being – Ahriman – to account for the flaws in creation. Ahriman was a dark creator spirit who had chosen evil and then become involved inextricably in the material world of light ruled by his good brother, Ahura Mazda. This concept influenced the gradual biblical development of Satan (the angel sent by God to try the patience of Job) into a fallen angel whose pride led him to choose evil and become God's direct adversary.

The most popular Christian image of Satan, partly borrowed from Greek depictions of the horned Minotaur and the goatish god Pan, shows him with horns, cloven hoofs and forked tail. He may be disguised as a monk, but a visible claw or hoof shows his true identity.

WITCHES AND WITCHING SYMBOLS

In western Europe from the 13th to 18th centuries, the witch became a prevailing symbol of the misuse of supernatural powers. Before this time, and in primitive societies generally, witches were feared and distrusted but their services were often sought.

Witchcraft became a hazardous occupation when people began to look on witches not as free agents but as servants of a powerful Devil. The Biblical invocation to "not permit a sorceress to live" was taken literally as late as 1692, when nineteen "convicted" witches were hanged in the Massachusetts Bay colony of Salem. While traditions of plural divinities accommodated hag goddesses, such as the Hindu Kali, as part of a dualistic natural order, in monotheistic Christianity, Satan was an error in nature whose followers had to be burnt. At the height of witch-hunting hysteria, witches became scapegoats for natural misfortunes, such as crop failure, madness or ideas unacceptable to the Church, including heresy or female lust.

Horace described Roman necromancy involving the slaughter of a black lamb. This reverse symbolism is typical of most traditional witching symbols. They include nocturnal animals (such as black cats, and owls); toads; wolves or (in Japan) foxes; goatlike symbols of lust; snakes; poisonous herbs; and such fearful sacrificial offerings as dead babies. Jung saw witches as projections of the dark side of the anima – the female side of human nature.

Magic

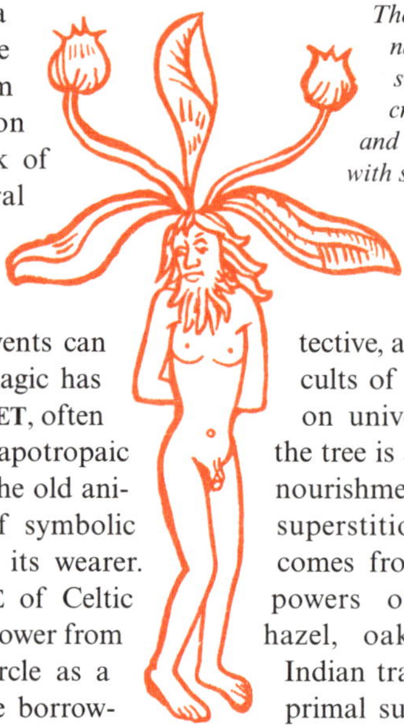

The mandrake, a Mediterranean narcotic plant with a forked root suggesting the human form, was credited with magical powers and became a symbol associated with sorcery and witchcraft.

Magic preceded religion as a means of seeking to influence the forces that help or harm human beings. While religion eventually took over the task of interceding with supernatural beings, its symbolic links with magic continued for centuries. And at a popular level, the idea that natural events can be affected by sympathetic magic has never disappeared. The **AMULET**, often made from amber or another apotropaic gem, is only one example of the old animist belief that an object of symbolic power (a stone) can protect its wearer. Similarly, the **ROUND TABLE** of Celtic and Hindu legend derives its power from ancient symbolism of the circle as a space imitating, and therefore borrowing force from, the cosmos itself.

The **HORSESHOE** is another ancient protective symbol. The tradition of showing it with the heel uppermost suggests that its supposed magic relied on the protective symbolism of the horned moon, the iron forming a crescent shape. **WOOD** is also protective, a symbolism based on early cults of beneficial tree spirits and on universal traditions in which the tree is an expression of maternal nourishment and the life force. The superstition of touching wood comes from the supposed magical powers of ash, hawthorn, hazel, oak and willow. In Indian tradition, wood is the primal substance shaping all things – Brahma.

The **BROOM** is a modest implement invested with magical power from ancient times. Essentially a symbol of removal ("the new broom sweeps clean"), it was superstitiously used with some care in case it drove out friendly spirits as well as dust. This fear explains folk prohibitions on sweeping a house at night in Brittany and, in North Africa, on sweeping a house in which someone has just died. The belief that witches rode brooms is linked to the idea that evil spirits could possess the magical implements used to drive them out.

The runic alphabet acquired magic symbolism as it spread to Scandinavia and was used to name sky gods. Belief that runes embodied supernatural powers led to their use in fortune-telling.

RITUAL DANCE

Dance is an instinctive expression of the life force, probably predating drawing and painting as a form of sympathetic magic. Primitive dancers, feeling themselves united with the flow of cosmic energy, believed that dance movements, patterns and gestures could influence the processes of nature or the unseen forces that control them.

This belief underlies the complex symbolism of ancient dance forms intended to invoke rain or sun, crop or human fertility, military success or the healing of disease, the protection of benign spirits or the appeasement of destructive ones. Because the acting out through dance of tribal beliefs or impending events – such as a hunt – induced group support, it seemed reasonable to suppose that it encouraged the help of the gods. Dance became the earliest form of theatre, translating religious dogma into expressive movement. Military victory was commonly rehearsed in war dances – the symbolism behind the sword dances of the Pathans or the Scots. Round dances mimicked the apparent movements of the sun, moon, or the seasons, while dancing around an object concentrated its energy or had protective symbolism. Shamans whirled like planets, arms raised to draw cosmic energy downward or lowered to direct it into the earth.

Dances with animal costumes, masks and miming similarly drew on the powers ascribed to different creatures. The serpentine dance of the priestess at Delphi drew on snake symbolism of wisdom and fertility. Union is symbolized by wedding dances and many forms of linked dancing; grief by funeral dances. In Africa and elsewhere, shaman healers sought to invoke and reinforce curative energies by dancing. The loss of individual consciousness involved in

A shaman dressed to symbolize death dances to frighten off evil spirits at a harvest festival in the Himalayan state of Bhutan.

uninhibited dancing can symbolize the attainment of a supernatural state in which the dancer is supposedly in direct touch with cosmic energy – a link made clear in the iconography of dancing gods. Shiva, the Hindu Lord of the Dance, often shown surrounded by flames, dances as the embodiment of both creative and destructive energy. In social or recreational dancing, and especially in folk dancing, which has direct links with fertility rites, the symbolism of a return to the vital centre of cosmic energy has dwindled but not disappeared.

Rituals

Magic merges with ritual in society's attempts to dramatize the passage from one life stage to another. Trials involved in **INTITATION CEREMONIES** symbolize the death of the old self, followed by birth of the new. **CIRCUMCISION**, an ancient ritual, widespread outside northern Europe, Mongolia and Hindu India, has both initiatory and sacrificial meanings in addition to any physical ones. The Hebrew commandment to circumcise males eight days after birth seems to have had both hygienic and symbolic importance, initiating children into a community chosen by God. Elsewhere, circumcision at puberty is a rite of passage to adulthood, often for females as well as males. An even earlier sacrificial symbolism has been suggested,

Dragon rain dances in Singapore show that ceremonies that have outworn their symbolism can still draw communities together.

PRIMEVAL CHAOS

Although ritual is now associated with disciplined and conventional forms of behaviour, this was by no means always the case in ancient societies. Apart from specific orgiastic cults, many early cultures institutionalized periods of licence in which social norms were rejected or even reversed.

In Babylonia, twelve days of anarchy acted out a mythical struggle against the chaos goddess in order to establish cosmic order. The Roman Saturnalia was similarly an authorized seven-day celebration at the December solstice to celebrate the rebirth of the vegetation god with a period of amusement and mild anarchy. These primitive revels may lie behind more recent traditions of carnival, which was originally held on Shrove Tuesday – popularly known in France as Mardi Gras (Fat Tuesday).

The symbolism of the religious orgy, as in the frenzied alcoholic rites of the Greek god Dionysus, was the annihilation of the difference between the human state – limited by time, morality, social convention or physical stamina – and the timeless, unlimited, ever-energized state of divinity.

The revel depicted in this Roman wall painting vividly captures the spirit of orgy as a symbolic tribute to the elemental creative forces of instinct and passion.

such that circumcision stands for a blood offering – a significant part of the body set aside in the hope of immortality. An alternative supposition is that circumcision, male and female, was an attempt to clarify sexual differences, the prepuce being seen as a feminine aspect of males, the clitoris as a masculine aspect of females.

When the Christian religion broke away from Judaism, the sacramental rite of **BAPTISM** effectively replaced the initiatory symbolism of circumcision, which was no longer prescribed. Symbolizing purification and regeneration, baptism represents dissolution of the old self and rebirth from the original waters of life. Cultic baptism was ancient and widespread – sometimes as a rite of initiation for the dead rather than the living. Depending on the denomination, Christian baptism can symbolize entry into the Church, an adult seal of faith, rebirth in grace, atonement for past sin, or symbolic sharing in the death and resurrection of Christ.

In many cultures **WASHING** has also been made into an important purification rite. Symbolically, it is an inner rather than outer cleansing – as in the Islamic custom of washing the face, hands and feet before thrice-daily worship. In Buddhist initiation ceremonies, novice monks ritually wash away their past lives. By ceremonially washing his hands after his trial of Christ, Pilate sought to absolve himself of any guilt for the Crucifixion.

Religious and social rituals of spirit or ancestor worship gave rise to haunting forms of Melanesian art, such as this New Guinea mask made of painted bark cloth and grasses.

OIL as well as water had symbolic significance in ritual practices from an early time, particularly in the Middle East. In the custom of anointing rulers or those undergoing priestly ordination, oil was used as a symbol of divine grace. The associations between oil and spiritual grace, illumination or benediction seem to have originated in the Middle East because olive oil was used there both to provide light and nourishment and as a medicinal balm.

Funerary rituals are laden with symbolic significance. **CREMATION**, for example, symbolized purification, sublimation and ascension for ancient Indo-Iranian peoples. Similar associations underlay cremation in western Europe from the Bronze Age, later spreading through the Roman Empire, often as a mark of high status. Dissolution of the body in fire symbolizes the freeing of the soul from the flesh and its ascension in smoke. Burial was preferred where doctrines of bodily resurrection were popular, such as in Egypt and Christian Europe.

Marriage

Few human rituals are more important and laden with symbolism than marriage. For millennia, marriage has been seen as a rite of passage in which the couple attain a semi-divine state of wholeness – the union of opposing male and female principles necessary to create and protect new life. The depiction in myth and art of the "marriage" of key dualities (gods and goddesses, sun and moon, heaven and earth, king and queen or, in alchemy, sulphur and mercury) symbolized the continuation of cosmic order, a process in which human marriages were felt to be important religiously as well as socially. The idea of human-divine union was often expressed in the terminology of marriage, as when nuns were called "brides of Christ".

Wedding customs were once full of symbolic meanings, the significance of which is now largely forgotten. Most were centred upon the bride in an attempt to ensure that marriages were fruitful as well as happy and legally binding. Binding symbols still in use include the **RING** (a circular symbol of eternity, union and completeness); the joining of **HANDS**; and the tying of **KNOTS**. In Hindu custom the bridegroom knots a ribbon around the neck of the bride, and the marriage sacrament, *vivaha*, is further made legal and binding by a formal seven-step dance designed to symbolize perfect marital harmony and cooperation.

This wedding motif combines four traditional symbols: the clasped hands of union, the pomegranate of fertility and ears of corn signifying prosperity and rebirth, all within the enclosing circle of continuity.

Wedding fertility symbols with an ancient history include the sprinkling of **GRAIN** or **RICE** over the couple – confetti is the modern sustitute. The **WEDDING CAKE** was once itself a fertility symbol (food being a sexual symbol). Its formal sharing during the wedding feast was also a symbolic means of uniting the two families and their close friends. Sympathetic fertility magic lies behind the custom of small children attending the bride, often elaborately costumed and carrying **FLOWERS** as further symbols of femininity and fruitfulness. Successful defloration of the virgin bride was magically ensured by the breaking of **GLASSES** or other objects.

The tradition of carrying the bride over the **THRESHOLD** survives from many different ceremonies surrounding the arrival of the bride at her marital house and her symbolic entry into a new life. Chinese brides used to step over a **SADDLE** at the gateway of the husband's parental home, a custom based on the similar sound of the words "saddle" and "peace".

Many other customs were devised to ward off evil influences, ensure luck, or act out social tensions caused by the marriage. Even a custom as apparently novel as tying cans to the back of the couple's car is the modern version of ancient magical tactics to drive away harmful spirits by making as much noise as possible.

Perugino's Marriage of the Virgin *is carefully composed to present a graceful image of symmetry, harmony and order – qualities that Renaissance society wanted to symbolize in the wedding ceremony.*

Offerings

From the earliest times, **SACRIFICE** represented a means of communion with divine beings in which something prized was sanctified and then destroyed as a symbolic offering. The high status and value of domestic animals in the ancient world made them the most common sacrifices, but offerings ranged from elaborate rituals of atonement or purification to funerary customs in which human victims were killed. At its deepest level, sacrifice was a creative act mimicking the death of all living things, particularly vegetative life in winter, as a necessary prelude to rebirth or the renewal of fertility. A savage example is the Aztec ritual in which victims were flayed alive to imitate the process by which the husks of maize cobs are shed. Similarly, in the practice of **DISMEMBERMENT** humans or animals were torn apart to symbolize the process of disintegration that leads to regeneration – paralleling the hacking down and harvesting of crops.

A gentler form of offering to the gods was the burning of **INCENSE**, a symbol of purity, virtue, sweetness and ascending prayer. Sacred literature and iconography suggest that incense was used originally to perfume sacrifices or funeral pyres but was later burned by itself as a purely symbolic offering, sharing the emblematic meaning of smoke as a visible link between earth and sky, humanity and divinity. Frankincense and myrrh, two of the gifts of the Magi after Christ's birth, were highly valued commodities throughout the ancient Middle East. In the civilizations of Egypt, Persia and the Sumerian-Semitic world, and later in Greece and Rome, these and other forms of incense were burned in daily worship. Farther east, in India, China and Japan, basil and sandalwood were widely used. (Joss-sticks is a pidgin English term for sticks of sandalwood, "joss" being a probable corruption of the Portuguese *deos*, meaning "god".)

The familiar **SCAPEGOAT** was originally another form of offering to the gods – a symbolic discharger of other people's sins

This Arabic illustration depicts a procession at the end of Ramadan, the 29-day sunrise-to-sunset Islamic fast. Like the Jewish Yom Kippur and the Christian Lent, it has penitential symbolism.

or shortcomings. A "goat for Azazel" (a desert demon) was sent into the wilderness by the Hebrews on the Day of Atonement (Yom Kippur), emblematically bearing away the transgressions of the Israelites. In Christianity, Christ made himself a scape-goat by taking on himself the sins of the world. According to J. G. Frazer in *The Golden Bough* (1890), earlier traditions in Asia Minor involved the beating and burning of a human victim as a scapegoat for the ruler in countries afflicted by drought, plague or crop failure.

Priests of the Aztec vegetation god Xipe Totec, depicted in this stone mask, wore the skins of flayed victims to symbolize the bursting of the husk enclosing seed.

Self-denial can also be a form of offering, as in **FASTING**, widely used in religion to symbolize penance, purification or worship. In Hinduism, Jainism and Taoism, the symbolism of fasting is purification and the creation of a physical state conducive to spiritual visions.

FLAGELLATION, when self-inflicted, is another symbol of penance, purification, discipline or sacrificial worship. Known from ancient times in many cults and religions, flagellation became so popular among Christian sects between the 11th and 15th centuries that it was proscribed as heretical behaviour.

PILGRIMAGE

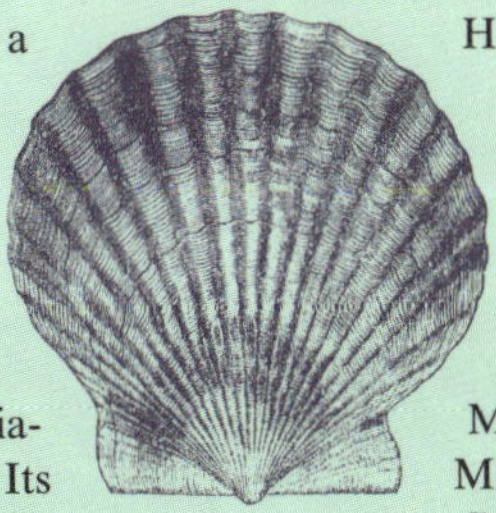

In many religions, undertaking a journey to a spiritual centre represents a form of offering that symbolizes expiation, purification, or ascension to a new plane of existence. In an emblematic sense, the pilgrimage is as much an initiation as an act of devotion. Its rationale is the ancient belief that supernatural forces manifest themselves most powerfully at particular localities. In the Islamic faith, the location is Mecca, birthplace of the Prophet. In Hinduism it is Benares on the Ganges. For Buddhists and Christians it is key sites in the life of Gautama Buddha and Christ. When the Holy Land fell under Islamic rule, the focus of huge Christian pilgrimages shifted to the shrines of saints, notably in Rome (associated with Peter and Paul) and in Santiago de Compostela (James, the son of Zebedee). More recently the cult of the Virgin Mary has again shifted Roman Catholic pilgrimages to places where she is said to have appeared and where miraculous cures are expected. Traditional symbols of the Western pilgrim include the bowl, broad-brimmed hat, cowl, gourd or flask, palm leaves (signifying a visit to Palestine), sack, scallop shell (the attribute of St James of Compostela) and staff.

Virtues and Sins

Many cultures have codified sins and virtues, but few display the symbolic wealth of Western Christendom. Greatest of the Pauline virtues was **CHARITY**, represented – like most virtues in Western art – by a young woman. She may hold a bundle of clothes for the naked, food for the hungry, or a flame, candle or flaming heart.

FAITH is another Pauline virtue, personified by a woman with a cross, chalice or candle. She is often shown standing at a font or with her foot on a cube. Third of the Pauline virtues is **HOPE**, a woman with anchor and a sailing ship as headdress. She may carry a basket of flowers or stretch out toward a crown. Fish, bread and wine were associated with hope in Hebrew tradition.

Of the cardinal virtues, **FORTITUDE** often appears as a warlike female, wearing nothing more than a helmet and shield and sometimes accompanying a lion or forcing its jaws apart. Other symbols are the camellia, carp, club, pillar and sword.

JUSTICE is represented by the figure of a blindfolded woman holding scales of judgment and a sword of power. Baroque artists who added the blindfold intended to show that Justice is unswayed by appearances. A snake or dragon accompanies **PRUDENCE**, who carries a mirror symbolizing self-knowledge, and hence wisdom. **TEMPERANCE**, another cardinal virtue, is often depicted pouring water from one pitcher into another (diluting wine). **CHASTITY**, personified most famously by the unicorn, can appear as a veiled figure, often carrying a shield (against the arrows of desire) or treading on a pig (lust). Other symbols of chastity are legion, among them the colours blue and white, bees, castles, chestnuts, crescents, crystals, diamonds, doves, elephants, enclosed gardens, ermine, girdles, hawthorns, irises, jade, laurel and lilies.

Justice is symbolized in Egyptian iconography by Osiris, who carries a flail and crook as emblems of his divine authority and his specific power to judge the dead.

The ermine is a symbol of chastity in Leonardo da Vinci's portrait. Its white winter coat was linked with purity because legend held that the animal would die if its coat was sullied.

THE SEVEN DEADLY SINS

A popular subject of Western art, particularly in the Renaissance and Baroque periods, the so-called "deadly" sins represented ordinary human failings rather than real evil.

ANGER is often represented as a woman tearing up her clothes. More interesting for artists was **AVARICE**, usually symbolized by a sinner holding or wearing a purse, or by a harpy attacking a miser hoarding money or golden apples. Among the other symbols of avarice are the rat and toad.

ENVY is often portrayed as a woman eating the heart torn from her own breast (the origin of the colloquialism "eat your heart out") or sometimes her entrails. Her familiar attribute is a snake, sometimes shown as her protruded, poisonous tongue. Other symbols of envy include the scorpion, the "evil eye" and the colour green (hence "green with envy"). **GLUTTONY** is personified either by corpulent and voracious figures or by the animals most commonly linked with this fleshly vice – notably the pig, bear, fox and wolf.

The preferred sinful subject for many medieval artists was **LUST**. Common symbols are snakes or toads, often shown feeding on the breasts or genitals of women (whose sexual urges seemed more shocking to the Church than those of men). The many other emblems of lust include the ape, ass, basilisk, bear, boar, cat, centaur, cock, Devil, goat, hare, horse, leopard, Minotaur and witch. **PRIDE** is usually personified by a woman with a peacock. She may also be shown with a lion and an eagle as dominant emblems of earthly and celestial nature. The biblical saying "pride goes before destruction and an haughty spirit before a fall" (Proverbs 16:18) led to medieval allegories of pride as an unseated horseman. This symbolism influenced Caravaggio's masterpiece *The Conversion of St Paul* (*c*.1600) showing Saul thrown from a horse on the road to Damascus. Other symbols of pride are the cock, fallen angel, leopard, mirror and ziggurat. **SLOTH** is often symbolized by a pig or an overweight man riding a beast of burden, such as the ass or ox. The snail was also a Christian emblem of sloth.

The Seven Deadly Sins depicted on a table top painted by Hieronymus Bosch, c.*1475–80. Christ looks on reproachfully at the centre of the table.*

The Animal World

Animals have always been the most immediate, powerful and important foundation for symbol systems of all cultures. No other source has provided such a varied range of iconography because there are few human qualities that cannot be represented in animal form. Psychology has followed religion in attaching to animals the essential symbolism of the instinctual, the unconscious, the libido and the emotions.

The reverence paid to animals in most primitive cultures had to do with a perception that they are more in touch with unseen cosmic forces than humankind. Their superior physical and sensory abilities led to the belief that they possessed magical or spiritual powers, and these powers could be accessed through animal rituals. Clans or tribes adopted them as totems for similar reasons, and skins, furs or feathers were worn to symbolize magical alliances in which animals were the patrons of the wearers. Most Egyptian gods were personified by animals, and elsewhere the most prestigious animals symbolized spiritual qualities.

The giant totem poles of America's northwest coast serve as tribal status symbols. This carved and painted thunderbird represents not only a mighty god but a mythical ancestral spirit symbolizing qualities that the clan admired and hoped to inherit.

Supernatural and Hybrid Beasts

The satyr, seen here grappling with a maenad, is a goatish symbol of male lust and the life of sensual pleasure. In classical mythology, satyrs accompany nature gods but medieval Christianity associated them with evil.

Imaginary beasts appear worldwide in myth and folklore as symbols of supernatural power or as compelling projections of the human psyche. Their precise symbolism often changed as their forms evolved. For example, the **SPHINX** was originally – in Egypt – a monumental human-headed lion that symbolized the power and majesty of the sun and the eternal glory of the ruler whom it commemorated. This is very different from the riddle-spinning sphinx of Greek invention, with its wings, female head and breasts, which Carl Jung saw as a symbol of the devouring mother. Likewise, the **GRIFFIN**, a lion-eagle emblem of dominion over land and sky, evolved from an aggressive emblem of power into a protective symbol.

The poisonous **BASILISK** snake turned into a medieval symbol of lust and disease with the addition of a cock's body and wings. Other frightening hybrids include **AMAMET** (a beast with a crocodile's jaw, a lion's mane and a hippopotamus' body), which devoured damned Egyptian souls, and the snake-maned Greco-Roman hellhound, **CERBERUS**. Both personify the fearful uncertainties of death. In Greek myth the **HYDRA**, a dragon-serpent with many heads, symbolizes the difficulty in conquering one's vices; each time one of its heads was chopped off, two grew back. **PEGASUS**, the winged horse of legend that carried the hero Bellerophon to victory over the fire-breathing **CHIMERA**, a snake-lion-goat hybrid, is a symbol of the victory of spirit over matter. Human-animal hybrids usually represent the animal-spiritual duality of human nature. Thus, the man-horse **CENTAUR** symbolizes man trapped by his own sensual impulses, especially lust and violence. The hybrid probably mythologized drunken bands of horsemen from the mountains of Thessaly, a region of East Central Greece on the Aegean coast.

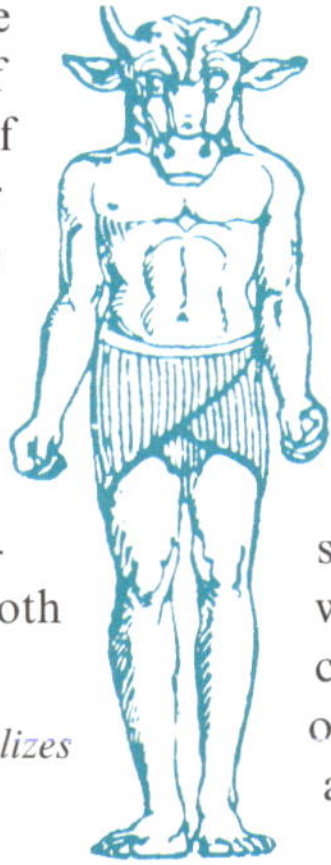

The bull-headed Cretan Minotaur symbolizes the tyranny of animal instinct and the destructiveness of repressed lusts.

The **LAMIA**, a snake-bodied devourer of other women's children, is a Greek symbol for jealousy, while the **GORGONS** (with hair of snakes, boars' teeth and gold wings) are more straightforward embodiments of adversarial evil. Some hybrids symbolize divine omnipotence, such as the goatfish **CAPRICORNUS**, which for the Sumerians depicted the creator god Ea. The elemental powers of nature called up other beasts of awesome size, such as the **LEVIATHAN** and **BEHEMOTH**.

THE EVOLUTION OF THE PHOENIX

The phoenix is the most famous of all rebirth symbols – a legendary bird that endessly renews itself in fire. The phoenix legend had its origin in the city of Heliopolis, ancient centre of Egyptian sun worship, where sacrifices were made to the heronlike Benu as the creative spirit of the sun. Based on these fire rituals and on descriptions of more gorgeous exotic birds, such as the golden pheasant, Greek writers wove stories which vary in detail but have an overall coherence. The phoenix (a word applied to the solar palm tree as well as to the bird) was a unique male bird of miraculous longevity – 500 years, or more by some accounts. At the end of this period, the phoenix built an aromatic nest, immolated itself, was reborn after three days, and carried the nest and ashes of its previous incarnation to the altar of the sun in Heliopolis.

Initially a myth based on the cyclic disappearance and reappearance of the sun, the phoenix soon became an emblem of human resurrection – and eventually of the indomitable human spirit in overcoming trials. Because artists were never quite sure what it looked like, its iconography is easily confused with the general solar (and soul) symbolism of other birds – especially with the eagle released from the pyre of a Roman emperor.

On Roman coins the phoenix symbolized the undying empire. It appears in early Christian funerary sculpture as a symbol of Christ's resurrection and the hope of victory over death. In medieval paintings it represents the divine nature of Christ when paired with the pelican. The phoenix can also appear as an attribute of Charity. A common motif in alchemy, it symbolizes the purifying and transforming fire, the chemical element sulphur, and the colour red.

Analogies are often made between the phoenix and other fabled birds, such as the Chinese Feng-Huang, shown here on the lacquered back of a Tang dynasty mirror. The bird symbolizes conjugal interdependence, combining solar and lunar forces.

Lords of Sacrifice

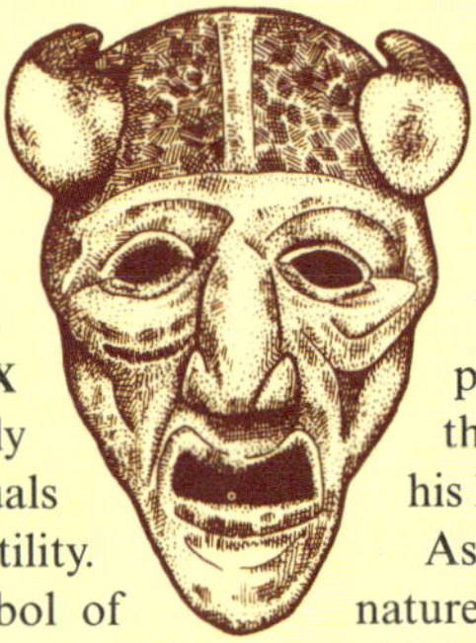

In North America, the animal most comparable with the bull as a symbol of divine power is the buffalo, shown here in a Cherokee wooden mask.

The sacrificial status of beasts in the ancient world was linked directly with their physical power and economic value, making the bull preeminent. But as the power that drove the ancient plough, the **OX** was also often used as a costly sacrifice, especially in cultic rituals connected with agricultural fertility. A universally benevolent symbol of strength, patience, submissiveness and steady toil, the ox is a Christian emblem of the sacrificial Christ and also of St Luke and of the priesthood generally. Now identified with slow-witted brawn, the epithet was once applied by Albertus Magnus to his bulky but formidably intelligent student Thomas Aquinas (1226–1274), who was to become one of the greatest philosophers of his era: "One day the dumb ox will fill the world with his lowing."

As an image of humanity's animal nature mastered, the ox is a Taoist and Buddhist attribute of the sage and of contemplative learning in China. The white ox was a forbidden food in several traditions. In the classical world, white oxen were sacrificed to the Greek god Zeus (in Roman myth, Jupiter) and black ones to Hades (Pluto). Black oxen pull the chariot of Death in art and are also an attribute of Night. Lunar associations often distinguish the ox from the solar bull.

The high status of the **BUFFALO** in India and southeast Asia made it a sacrificial animal. Yama, the Hindu and Buddhist god of death rode a black buffalo, and a buffalo head was a death symbol in Tibet. The Chinese associated the quiet power of the domestic buffalo with the contemplative life. In legend, the sage Lao-tse left China on a green buffalo.

The North American buffalo (actually a **BISON**) symbolized to the Plains Indians not only the strength of the whirlwind but also prosperity, plenty and supernatural power. The white buffalo was particularly sacred, and their slaughter by white hunters outraged the Plains Indians.

With the ass, the ox is the beast most often depicted in paintings of the Nativity. Also, it sometimes appears supporting baptismal fonts.

THE BULL AS ICON AND ADVERSARY

The bull is not only a dominant animal symbol but it also had extraordinary emblematic significance as a sacrifice. In ritual and iconography, it has represented both moon and sun, earth and sky, rain and heat, feminine procreation and male ardour, matriarch and patriarch, death and regeneration. As a symbol of death and resurrection, it was central to Mithraism, a pre-Zoroastrian Persian cult taken up and spread through much of the Roman empire as an early rival to Christianity. In the Roman *taurobolium*, initiates showered under bull's blood as a stream of life. Similar germination symbolism appears in much older Indo-Iranian myths. In still earlier cave art, the bull is second only to the horse as the most frequently painted image of vital energy. It appears from northern Europe through to India as an emblem of divine power, especially associated with lunar, solar and sky or storm gods. In condemning the Golden Calf, the biblical Moses sought to change a long tradition of Semitic bull worship.

In India, the first saint of the ascetic Jain sect is represented by a golden bull. Physical attributes of the bull underlie much of its symbolism. Its horns are linked with the crescent moon, its sheer bulk suggests a support for the world in Vedic and Islamic traditions, its prolific semen is stored by the moon in Persian mythology, and its bellowing, stamping, horn-tossing energy is widely linked with thunder and earthquakes, especially in Crete, home of the monstrous mythological bull-man, the Minotaur.

As the most formidable of all domesticated beasts, the bull became an adversary as well as icon from ancient times. Challenging its power was a task given to legendary heroes, such as Hercules – and a dangerous game for Minoan acrobats who somersaulted over the bull's horns.

The orchestrated ritual of modern bull-fighting continues a long tradition of using the bull to flirt with death. Here, the straightforward symbolism of cheating death is perhaps more fundamental than Jung's moralizing view that the defeat of the bull represents a human wish to sublimate animal passions. However, sexual symbolism is certainly prominent in Greek mythology, witnessed by the link with the orgiastic rites of Dionysus and by the myth in which Zeus appears to Europa as a gentle white bull, before abducting her. Diodorus reported that Egyptian women exposed themselves to images of the Apis bull. However, death and resurrection symbolism, as found in Mithraism, is more widespread: it is very marked in Egypt and also in northern Asia, where Death rides a black bull.

Mithras slaughters a primordial bull from whose blood and semen spring new life.

Horses and Deer

An archetypal symbol of animal vitality, velocity and beauty, the **HORSE** was also linked with conquest and superiority in many cultures – hence the popularity of the equestrian statue as an emblem of mastered power. In cave art, as in Romantic painting, horses flow across the surface medium like incarnations of the force of life itself. They can represent the elemental powers of wind, storm, fire, waves and running water. As a symbol of the continuity of life, a horse was sacrificed to Mars, the Roman god of war and agriculture, each October. Its tail was kept throughout the winter as a fertility emblem.

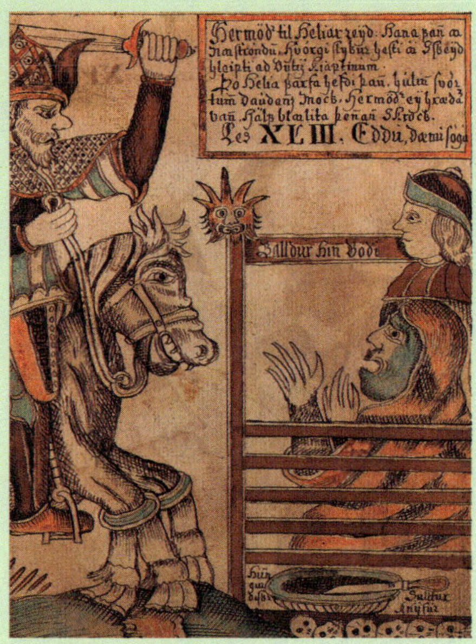

Sleipnir, the mare of the Norse sky god Odin, has eight legs in mythology, symbolizing the combined power and speed of the eight winds.

In ancient belief, horses knew the mysteries of the underworld, the earth and its cycles of germination. This early chthonic symbolism was replaced by a more widespread association of the horse with sun and sky gods, although horses continued to play a part in funerary rites as guides or messengers in the spirit world. The riderless horse is still used as a poignant symbol in military and state funerals.

Death is often shown riding a black horse. The white horse is almost invariably a solar symbol of light, life and spiritual illumination. It is an emblem of the Buddha (said to have left his worldly life on a white horse), of the Hindu Kalki (the last incarnation of Vishnu), of the merciful Bato Kannon in Japan, and of the Prophet in Islam (for whom horses are emblems of happiness and wealth). Christ is sometimes shown riding a white horse. The winged horse is similarly a solar or spiritual symbol. Horses draw the chariot of the sun in classical, Iranian, Babylonian, Indian and Nordic mythology. Although predominantly linked with elemental or instinctual powers, horses can symbolize the speed of thought. Legend and folklore often invest them with magical powers of divination.

Deer antlers represent spring fertility, prosperity and fecundity in this image of the Celtic antlered god Cernunnos, an emblem of crop growth.

DEER are also linked with supernatural powers. The Northern Germanic idea that reindeer were associated with the winter solstice led to the folkloric belief that reindeer pull the sleigh of Santa Claus (St Nicholas – a 4th-century bishop, whose fame for generosity derives from his gifts of dowries to poor girls). Deer are universally benevolent symbols, associated with the East, dawn, light, purity, regeneration, creativity and spirituality. The **STAG** or hart is a solar emblem of fertility, its branching antlers suggesting in Native American and other traditions the Tree of Life, the sun's rays and, through their shedding and regrowth, longevity and rebirth.

The unicorn symbolized the virtue of pure love and the power of a chaste woman to tame and transform the horn of sexual desire.

The stag is linked with virility and ardour and, particularly in China, with wealth and happiness. The ten-pointed antlers of the shaman were an emblem of supernatural powers. The **ANTELOPE** is another symbol of grace and speed – a spiritual ideal and fit mount for gods in both African and Indian traditions. In the sublimated form of the **UNICORN** it became the leading emblem of Chastity – a courtly symbol of sublimated desire and a Christian symbol of the Incarnation.

THE MISUNDERSTOOD ASS

Although the ass or donkey has now become a well-entrenched emblem of foolishness, its symbolism is traditionally more various and positive than this. Christ chose a donkey colt for his entry into Jerusalem both to fulfil a prophecy and to signify the virtue of meekness. As a result, the donkey stands for humility, patience and poverty in Christian thought. Chinese immortals ride white asses. By contrast, asses play harmful, even sinister, roles in both Egyptian and Indian myths, and are associated with lust or comical stupidity in Greco-Roman legends. In Ovid's famous tale, King Midas of Phrygia was foolish enough to prefer the pipes of Pan to the lyre of Apollo and was given the ears of an ass as a symbol of his musical and spiritual obtuseness. Folklore also associates the donkey with sloth and obstinacy.

Shakespeare satirized romantic folly in his play A Midsummer Night's Dream *by making Titania fall in love with Bottom wearing the comic mask of an ass.*

The Cultic Snake

A Greek image of a snake curled round an egg represents the world protected by a cosmic serpent.

Of all animal symbols, the **SNAKE** is the most significant and complex. Sexual or agricultural fertility symbolism appears to have been a basic element in early snake cults. But analogies between the snake and the penis, the umbilical cord or the humid processes of birth (for the snake combines male and female symbolism) do not alone explain the importance of the serpent in mythology. Almost universally, the snake was also a magico-religious symbol of primeval life force – and sometimes an image of the creator divinity itself. The motif of a snake swallowing its own tail symbolized not only eternity but a divine self-sufficiency.

Emblematically, the snake was in touch with the earth's mysteries, the waters, darkness and the underworld – self-contained, sometimes venomous, cold-blooded, highly secretive, able to glide swiftly without feet, magically swallow large creatures, and rejuvenate itself by shedding its own skin. Its serpentine form was as allusive as its other characteristics, suggesting undulating waves and landscapes, winding rivers, vines and tree roots, and in the sky the rainbow, the lightning strike, the spiralling motion of the cosmos. As a result, the snake became one of the most widespread of all animist symbols.

In mythology, the Hindu creator god Vishnu rests on the coils of a **GREAT SNAKE**, Ananta (Shesha); Indra slays a chaos snake, Vritra, to release the fertilizing waters it enclosed; and the great earthquake snake, Vasuki, is used to churn the

THE HEALING SNAKE

Paradoxically, the snake was often used as a curative symbol. Entwined snakes on the caduceus – the staff of Hermes (Mercury) symbolizing mediation between opposing forces – was interpreted by psychologist Carl Jung as an emblem of homeopathic medicine. The bronze serpent set up by Moses at God's suggestion to heal snakebites (Numbers 21:9) was a similar homeopathic emblem and was later taken to prefigure Christ on the cross, healing the sins of the world. A snake nailed to the cross in medieval Christian art is thus a symbol of resurrection and of spiritual sublimation of the physical life force. In the ancient world, the snake's rejuvenation symbolism linked it specifically with the classical god of healing, Aesculapius.

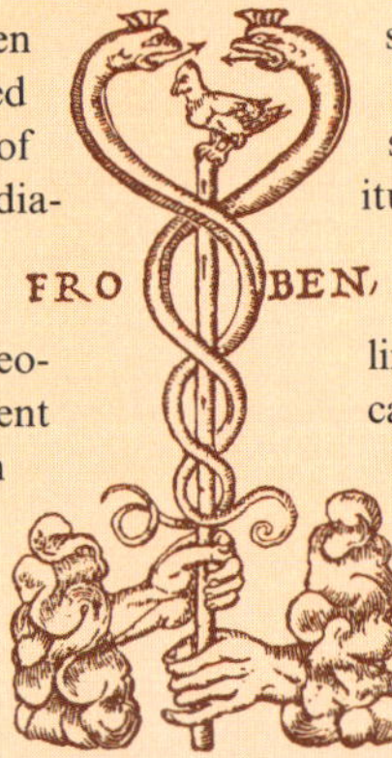

The caduceus, a rod entwined by two serpents and sometimes capped with wings, has always been an emblem of commerce as well as medicine.

Fertility symbolism is the likeliest explanation for ancient snake motifs, as in this Bronze Age scene carved on a Scandinavian rockface.

sea of creation. In African and other myths, a **RAINBOW SNAKE** reaches from the watery underworld into the heavens. In South America, eclipses were explained as the swallowing of the sun or moon by a giant serpent. The Aztec **BIRD-SNAKE** divinity Quetzalcoatl unites the powers of earth and heaven. In Egypt, the barque of the sun that travels through the underworld waters at night is threatened by the serpent Apep, and has to enter another great serpent to be reborn each morning.

The protective-destructive symbolism that runs through these and other serpent myths illustrates the degree to which the snake is a dualistic force, a source of strength when mastered but potentially dangerous and often emblematic of death or chaos as well as of life. A positive symbol of serpentine inner strength, psychic energy and latent spiritual power is the yogic *kundalini* coiled at the base of the spine. The snake in its more dangerous aspect is symbolized in both India and Egypt by the erect, hooded cobra. In Egypt, this forms the uraeus, a protective serpent emblem of royal power to strike down enemies. In India, **COBRA** divinities (Nagas) were guardian symbols, generally benevolent, as in the image of the seven-hooded cobra that shields the Buddha. Snakes often appear there and elsewhere as guardians of shrines, of sources of water or of treasure.

These traditions are linked with serpent fecundity symbolism and the superstition that precious stones were formed from snake saliva. The Hindu cobra is often shown with a jewel in its hood, symbolizing spiritual treasure. As in Africa and North America, snakes appear as both progenitor gods and ancestor figures in Chinese mythology; house snakes were thought to bring luck as forefather spirits. Ancestral symbolism, together with the belief that snakes understood earth mysteries and could see in the dark, help to account for the link between the serpent and wisdom or prophecy.

Psusennes I wears the pharaonic uraeus, or cobra diadem, on his silver coffin at Tanis.

Reptile Enemies

A Nepali gilded bronze shows a snake, representing the darkness of evil, being crushed by the Garuda, a legendary bird of light in Indian mythology.

The snake's duality – a balance between fear and veneration – accounts for its frequent appearance in symbolism as an enemy of humankind. In its fearful aspect, it gave birth to the **DRAGONS** and **SEA SERPENTS** of Western tradition and to **SNAKE HYBRIDS** that symbolized the multiple perils of human existence, typified by the children of Echidna in Greek legend – the Hydra, the Chimera and the snake-backed hell-hound Cerberus. At the level of Western folklore, the snake's symbolism is usually negative, its forked tongue suggesting hypocrisy or deceit, its venom bringing sudden and treacherous death. In Tibetan Buddhism the **GREEN SNAKE** of hatred is one of the three base instincts. The snake is one of the five noxious animals of China, although it appears in more positive roles too. The snake as Satan was foreshadowed in the dualistic Iranian religion of Zoroastrianism, which symbolized the serpent as a spirit of evil. In Germanic lore both Thor and Beowulf slay and are slain by dragon-serpents. It is tempting to see snake-slaying as a symbol of the destruction of a paternal or older power – as in the legend in which the Greek hero Herakles (Hercules) strangled two snakes in his cradle. To establish his cult at Delphi, Apollo had to kill Python, dragon nurse of the terrible monster Typhon – a myth that suggests the replacement of an older, maternal serpent cult. This may be the meaning of Baal's destruction of the seven-headed serpent Lotan in Phoenician myth.

In a context where too much knowledge was impious, the snake's wisdom was turned against it – as in the biblical story of how Eve was beguiled by a serpent "more crafty than any other wild animal that the Lord God had made" (Genesis 3:1). The snake wound around the forbidden tree in Eden has many parallels in the Middle East. A snake-entwined tree was an emblem of the fertility goddess Ishtar. As

In Greek myth a snake guards the golden apples of the Hesperides, as depicted in this painting by Sir Edward Burne-Jones.

shown by the many other earth goddesses who are depicted holding phallic snakes, serpents played important roles in vegetation fertility cults of the Mediterranean and Near East; Semitic fertility cults used them in sexual rites to approach the godhead. Eve's offer to Adam of the forbidden fruit (a symbol of an attempt to acquire divine powers) has been read as a Hebrew warning against the seductions of such rival cults. Hence the Judeo-Christian symbolism of the serpent as the enemy of humankind and its later identification with "that old serpent called the Devil" (Revelation 12:9). In Western art, the snake thus became a dominant symbol of evil, sin, temptation or deceit.

The hybrid Chimera is portrayed with a tail in the form of a snake to convey its fearful nature.

THE ARCHETYPAL DEVOURER

Of all reptiles, the crocodile is the leading symbol of destructive voracity – an agent of divine retribution, and lord of water and earth, life and death. Often an object of uninformed awe or moralizing hostility, the crocodile was believed by the Roman historian Plutarch to be worshipped in Egypt because it had the divine qualities of silence and the ability to see all with its eyes covered by membranous tissue. Where it was known, it was treated with fearful respect as a creature of primordial and occult power over water, earth and the underworld. In India it was the Makara, the fish-crocodile steed of Vishnu. In Egyptian iconography, the dead often appear as crocodiles and the town of Crocodopolis was dedicated to the crocodile fecundity god, Sebek. In more monstrous imagery, Amamet, who devoured the hearts of wrongdoers, had crocodile jaws, and the god Set took the form of a crocodile to devour his brother Osiris. In Native American iconography, the crocodile, or alligator, appears with open jaws as the nocturnal sun-swallower. Some Central American myths say that the crocodile gave birth to the earth or supports it on its back. Rebirth symbolism appears in Liberia where circumcision scars were said to be the marks of a crocodile that swallowed youths and returned them as adults. In the West, the crocodile is sometimes interpreted as a form of dragon. However, it has more positive water and earth symbolism in many parts of Asia, including China, where it appears as the inventor of the drum and song.

The crocodile's symbolic role as an enemy of man is made terrifyingly clear in this border pattern on a 16th-century ivory jug from Sierra Leone.

Dragon

The **DRAGON** is a reptilian creature so Mesozoic that the human imagination seems to have stretched back 70 million years to give it form. Because dragons are generally beneficent symbols in the Far East, malevolent in the West, their symbolism is not as straightforward as it might appear. In myth and legend, the dragon and **SERPENT** were often synonymous – in China, for example, and also in Greece where large snakes were called *drakonates*, a word suggesting sharp-sightedness (from *derkomai*, "to perceive keenly"). The association between the dragon and vigilance (which it can personify in art) is evidenced by many tales in which dragons appear as guardians linked with the underworld and with oracular knowledge. Christianity was the primary influence behind the evolution of the dragon into a generalized symbol of adversarial evil. The dragon of medieval imagination combines air, fire, water and earth symbolism. It is generally depicted as a fire-breathing, horned creature with eagle legs, bat wings, a scaly body and a serpentine, barbed tail (sometimes shown knotted to indicate its defeat). Alternatively, it appears as a **SEA SERPENT**, as in some paintings of St George, a tradition dating back to Sumerian-Semitic iconography of the chaos goddess Tiamat. The Greek hero Perseus also battled with an aquatic monster to save the princess Andromeda. Purely as an image of terror, the dragon was a popular emblem of warriors, appearing on Parthian and Roman standards, in the carved prows of Viking ships, in the Celtic world as a symbol of sovereign force, and on banners in Anglo-Saxon England, and in Wales, where the red dragon still remains as the national emblem.

Undulating across the surface of a Ming dynasty table, this dragon is a symbol of supernatural power untrammelled by moral disapproval.

In Asia, and particularly in China, it symbolizes the generative rhythms of the natural elements, particularly the rain-bearing power of thunder, often shown as a pearl held in the dragon's mouth or throat. Hence the rain symbolism of the paper dragons carried in processions amid fireworks in spring festivals on the second day of the second Chinese month. The turquoise **FIVE-CLAWED DRAGON** Lung was the motif of the Han dynasty and symbolized the active yang principle, the East, the rising sun, fertility, happiness and the gifts of spiritual knowledge and immortality. The **THREE-CLAWED DRAGON** is a symbol of the mikado in Japan, and a leading rain symbol there and elsewhere in southeast Asia, while with four claws the Chinese dragon stands for temporal power. The dragon has similar power symbolism in Indian tradition.

St George, here depicted in a painting by Raphael, is one of several Christian saints credited with killing a dragon – variously symbolizing disorder, unbelief, evil or primal bestiality. The Virgin Mary is also sometimes shown with a dragon underfoot, representing the conquest of evil.

Elephants, Apes, Bears and Boars

The **ELEPHANT** is an ancient symbol of sovereign power in China, Africa, and particularly India, where it was the stately mount not only of Indian rulers but of the thunder and rain god Indra. By association, the elephant came to symbolize not only the qualities required for good government – dignity, intelligence, prudence – but also a whole range of general benefits including peace, bountiful harvests and rainfall. Fertility and rainfall symbolism were particularly attached to the **WHITE ELEPHANT** in Burma, Thailand and Cambodia. The impending birth of the Buddha was announced to his mother, Queen Maya, by the dream that a charming little white elephant had entered her womb. For Buddhists the elephant is a symbol of spiritual knowledge as well as stability.

The elephant's Roman association with victory (it personifies Fame in art) may account for its occasional use as a symbol of Christ's overcoming death or evil. A medieval belief that the bull elephant refrained from sex during the long gestation period of his mate made it a Western symbol of chastity, fidelity and love.

The elephant's link with ponderous clumsiness appears to be modern, although there is a delightful Hindu legend that describes how elephants lost their powers of flight by being cursed by a hermit whose home in a banyan tree had been crushed on their landing.

The Indian elephant-headed god Ganesha symbolized wisdom in his role as patron of the art and craft of writing.

Elephant **IVORY** acquired its own symbolic value of incorruptibility. The symbolism of lofty aloofness (hence ivory towers) probably derives from the high status of ivory in ancient cultures, where it was used to produce some of the most durable of all works of art. Its Christian association with purity and, in particular, with the Virgin Mary is linked to its whiteness.

The **APE** is an animal of sharply diverging symbolism, respected in ancient Egypt, Africa, India and China, but deeply distrusted in Christian tradition where it was equated with vice, lust, idolatry and devilish heresies. Like the **MONKEY**, its imitative skills were widely used to satirize human vanity and other follies.

In Western art the ape appears with an apple in its mouth as a symbol of the Fall, and later more playfully as an analogue for artists themselves imitating nature. In Egyptian iconography the caped **BABOON** salutes the rising sun as the "hailer of the dawn" and is a symbol of wisdom. In Tibetan tradition, the Bodhisattva Avalokiteshvara (incarnate in the form of the Dalai Lama) originally entered the country in the guise of a saintly monkey. Stories and legends of monkey-kings appear in Chinese and Indian myth where they play agile, intelligent hero roles.

Viking boar helmets had aggressive symbolism, and were believed to put the wearer under the protection of the god Frey.

The wild **BOAR** was a primordial image of strength, fearless aggression and resolute courage, particularly across northern Europe and the Celtic world, where it also symbolized spiritual authority. Its meat was eaten ritually and buried with the slain. Small votive boars and larger stone boar sculptures have been found as far south as Iberia. The boar had sacred meaning, too, as a sun symbol in Iran and as a moon symbol in Japan, where white boars were taboo to hunters. Respect for the boar extended into India where the god Vishnu took on a boar's form to dive into the flood and root the earth up with his tusks after it had been captured by demons. However, the boar's ferocity aroused horror as well as respect. Associations between the boar and the destructive behaviour of warriors using it as an emblem made it a Christian symbol for tyranny and lust.

Hanuman, the Hindu monkey god, was a healer and warrior.

SYMBOLISM OF THE BEAR

As a symbol of primeval force, the bear was an incarnation of the god Odin in Scandinavia, where the fierce Berserkers wore bearskins into battle. It is linked with many other warlike divinities including the Greek mother goddess Artemis (whose cultic maidens were "bears"), the Germanic Thor and the Celtic Artio, whose worshippers included the people of Berne (Swiss city of "the bear"). The bear is also an emblem of masculine courage in China where dreams of a bear presaged the birth of sons. As a symbol of strength, the bear is an ancestral figure to the Ainu of northern Japan, and plays a similar role in the mythology of the Algonquin tribe of Native Americans. Elsewhere, it is sometimes linked with lunar and resurrection symbolism, perhaps because of its hibernation. Shamans used bear-masks to communicate with forest spirits. Although she-bears appear widely as symbols of maternal strength, care and warmth, Jung linked them with dangerous aspects of the unconscious. In Christian and Islamic traditions the bear is cruel, lustful and vengeful and it can represent gluttony in Western art.

A common totem among Native American tribes, the bear embodied the strength of the whirlwind.

Cats, Big and Small

The **LION** is the most commanding animal image of the great and terrible in nature, often personifying the power of the sun itself. Its solar associations were based on the iconographic splendour of its golden coat, radiant mane and sheer physical presence. It appears as both destroyer and saviour, invested with a godlike dualism and so capable of representing evil and its destruction. The theme of the royal lion hunt, common in the early iconography of western Asia, symbolized death and resurrection – the continuation of life ensured by the killing of a godlike animal. In some carvings the lion seems to offer itself for sacrifice and the king's own divinity is suggested by his fearless grasp of the animal's paws – an archetypal image of human courage matching lion courage.

This Tibetan bronze of a Bodhisattva seated on a lion refers to Indian descriptions of the Buddha as a lion among men.

In Egypt, the avenging goddess Sekhmet, represented as a lioness, symbolized the ferocious heat of the sun, but the lion was also a guide to the underworld. Hence the lion-footed tombs found in Egypt and images of mummies carried on lions' backs. Lion masks or ringed lion door knockers (symbols of eternity) were common on Egyptian doors. Egypt was also the origin of lion-headed water spouts or fountains, symbolizing the fertile flooding of the Nile when the sun was in the zodiacal sign Leo (July 23–August 22).

Victory over death is symbolized by the wearing of lion skins and by myths like that in which Herakles slays the Nemean lion or Samson tears a lion limb from limb. Alternatively, in Judaism the lion of death is overcome by prayer (Daniel in the lion's den). More widely, the lion is a symbol of royal power and dominion, military victory, bravery, vigilance and fortitude, a virtue personified in art by a woman grappling with a lion. The lion was a royal emblem of Scotland and England, and became a dominant symbol of British imperial power in the 19th century. In China and Japan, the lion is protective, lion-mask dances having the same purpose as dragon dances.

The leopard represented evil in ancient Egypt and in Christian tradition. Shamanic leopard skins symbolize mastery over the beast's demonic power.

In Asia and India, the **TIGER** largely replaces the lion as a symbol of the great and terrible in nature. Several gods show their power by riding them, and warriors used them as battle emblems. Protective symbolism accounts for the stone tigers on Chinese graves and doorways, and for the ancient custom by which children wear tiger caps.

In the symbolism of Central and South America, the dominant animal is the **JAGUAR** – linked with divination, royalty, sorcery, the forces of the spirit world, the earth and moon, and fertility. The belief that by transforming themselves into jaguars, shamans could command occult powers, was widespread, and accounts for the many images of snarling jaguar-human hybrids in Mesoamerican art from the Olmec period (*c.*1500–*c.*400BC) onward.

The jaguar, depicted here in a warrior role in the Aztec Codex, was an awesome incarnation of the supreme god Tezcatlipoca, whose magic mirror-eyes revealed all things from the thoughts of humans to the mysteries of the future.

THE FELINE ENIGMA

The small size of **DOMESTIC CATS** does not diminish their symbolic power. They represent transformation, clairvoyance, agility, watchfulness, sensual beauty, mystery and female malice. These almost universal associations had differing significance in ancient cultures. In Egypt, notably in the worship of the feline-headed goddess Bastet or Bast, cats were benign and sacred creatures. Bastet, originally shown as a lioness, was a tutelary lunar goddess, linked with pleasure, fertility and protective forces. In her honour, cats were venerated and often mummified, along with mice for them to eat. In iconography, the cat appeared as an ally of the sun, severing the head of the underworld serpent. Cats were also associated with other lunar goddesses, including the Greek Artemis (Diana to the Romans), and with the Nordic goddess Freya whose chariot they drew. In Rome their self-sufficient freedom also made them emblems of Liberty.

Elsewhere, their night wanderings and powers of transformation (pupil dilation, sheathing and unsheathing of claws, sudden changes from indolence to ferocity) were distrusted. **BLACK CATS** in particular, were linked with evil cunning in the Celtic world, with harmful *djins* in Islam, and with bad luck in Japan where folk tales described how cats could take over the bodies of women. In India, where cats embodied animal beauty, Buddhists seem to have held their aloofness against them: like the serpent, they failed to mourn the Buddha's death. The most negative view of all appears in the vast folklore of Western witchcraft where cats appear as demonic familiars associated with satanic orgies – lustful and cruel incarnations of the Devil himself.

Mummification of cats (and their food) was not uncommon in Egypt, where their use as household pets is known to date back at least 4,000 years.

Domestic Animals

Sheep-herding societies of the ancient world attached solar and fire symbolism to the **RAM**. As an emblem of solar energy, it represented potent gods including Amun-Ra in Egypt, Ea and Baal in the Middle East, Apollo in Greece, Indra and Agni in India. As the first sign of the zodiac, Aries the ram symbolizes the renewal of fertility and returning warmth of the sun at the March equinox. Rams can also symbolize virility, ardour and obstinacy. By contrast, **SHEEP** usually represent meekness and a helpless need for leadership and protection. Of far greater significance in Christian iconography is the **LAMB** – one of the earliest symbols of Christ, and an emblem of purity, sacrifice, renewal, redemption, innocence, gentleness, humility and patience. Emblematic use of the lamb in Christian iconography and scripture extended an already long Semitic tradition in which newborn lambs were sacrificed as symbols of spring renewal. The blood of the paschal lamb was, from the time of the Passover, a particular mark of Hebrew salvation, and prophets such as Isaiah described the coming Messiah as a lamb. The lamb is an important sacrificial and

THE ORIGINS OF THE DEVILISH GOAT

Much of the ambiguous symbolism of the goat resolves itself along sexual lines: virility, lust, cunning and destructiveness in the male; fecundity and nourishing care in the female. The goat Amaltheia was the revered wet-nurse of the Greek god Zeus (in Roman myth, Jupiter), her horn the cornucopia of abundance – symbolism soundly based on the quality and suitability of goat's milk for babies.

The goat was the mount of the ancient Vedic god Agni. This Persian image shows it as the zodiacal sign of Capricorn.

The vitality of the male goat impressed the ancient world, as its connection with several Sumerian-Semitic and Greek gods shows. It provided many of the physical features of Pan and the satyrs. Male goats are particularly active in winter (when the female comes on heat), which may account for images of straw goats used in Scandinavian corn festivals held at yuletide – a season sometimes personified by the goat. However, the goat's virility was seen by the Hebrews as lewd. The fifth century BC Greek historian Herodotus reported bestial sexual practices in the Mendesian cult of the goat among the Egyptians. This may have influenced Christian symbolism of the goat as a personification of impurity and vile lust – hence the goatish physical characteristics of the medieval Devil, an association strengthened by the goat's reputation for malicious destructiveness. Goats can also personify folly, but in China and India the goat is a positive masculine symbol.

redemptive symbol in the Islamic rites of Ramadan.

The spiral horns of the ram were an Egyptian emblem of the solar power of gods and rulers.

An ancient symbol of maternal nourishment, the **COW** often appears in cultures from Egypt to China as a personification of Mother Earth. It was also lunar and astral, its crescent horns representing the moon (as in images of the Egyptian cow goddess Hathor), its abundant milk the countless stars of the Milky Way. A similar image of the cow as the nourisher of original life appears in the mythology of northern Europe where Adumla, the bovine wet-nurse of the primordial giants, licks the ice to disclose the first man. To both Hindus and Buddhists, the cow's quiet, patient rhythms of life presented an image of holiness so complete that it became India's most sacred animal. Its image is everywhere one of happiness.

The symbolism of the **PIG** is less consistent. It can represent gluttony, selfishness, lust, obstinacy and ignorance – but also motherhood, fertility, prosperity and happiness. In early cultures, **SOWS** were venerated as Great Mother emblems of fecundity. The pig was a fertility and virility symbol in China. Jewish and Islamic distrust of eating scavengers' meat influenced more negative associations between pigs and animal passions like greed and lust.

The **COCK** can also personify lust in Western art, but in Christianity its symbolism is generally positive. Church weathervanes in the form of cocks are emblems of vigilance against evil. Roosters are linked with the dawn, the sun and illumination almost everywhere except in Celtic and Nordic traditions. In China, the cock exemplified the five virtues of civil and military merit, courage, reliability and generosity (from its practice of offering food to its hens). It was also a funerary emblem, warding off evil. Cocks were sacred animals in Japan, hence the free run they are given in Shinto temples. In Islamic tradition, a cock was the giant bird seen by Muhammad in the First Heaven crowing, "There is no God but Allah." Many African traditions associate the cock with secret knowledge and hence witchcraft.

The emblem of France because its Latin name also meant "Gaul", the cock hovers with the eagle of victory over the spirits of fallen French troops.

Dogs, Jackals and Wolves

Celtic and Christian traditions largely established the **DOG** as a symbol of loyalty and protective vigilance. The Dominicans were proud to be called "dogs of the Lord". In more primitive and ancient thought, the dog was associated almost universally with the underworld in which it acted as both guide and guardian. Their companionship in life and their supposed knowledge of the spirit world suggested dogs as suitable guides to the afterlife. They play this role even in in Central America where they carried Mayan souls across the river of death. Xoltl, the Aztec dog god, led the sun through the nocturnal underworld and was reborn with it at dawn. Dogs were often sacrificed as companions for the dead. They are guardian symbols in Japan, and also in China, although less consistently because they can have demonic significance, especially in the symbolism of cosmic disasters. Elsewhere, the dog or **COYOTE** often appears with divinatory symbolism or as a culture hero – especially in North America and Africa.

As an evil-smelling scavenger, the **JACKAL** symbolized destructiveness or evil in India. But in ancient Egypt it was equated with the dog and worshipped as Anubis, the god of embalming, who led souls to judgment. Anubis is commonly shown either as a black jackal or as a jackal-headed human figure.

The positive Christian symbolism of the dog appears in this painting of Saint Roch, a 14th-century hermit whose dog cared for him when he caught the plague. Dogs accompany healer goddesses in Celtic art.

The symbolism of the **WOLF** is equally inconsistent. Sometimes associated with cruelty, cunning and greed, it appears in other cultures as a symbol of courage, victory or nourishing care. In pastoral societies of the Middle East and in heavily wooded and populated regions of Europe, the wolf is a famous predatory creature. The big, bad wolf of folklore was both a devouring and sexually predatory symbol. Stories of witches turning into wolves and men into werewolves symbolized fears of demonic possession and of male violence and sadism. The wolf was sacred to Apollo in Greece and to Odin (Woden) in Nordic myth, where it was considered to be a bringer of victory (although Fenris, the cosmic wolf, was a harbinger of evil). The **SHE-WOLF** suckling Romulus and Remus (the children of Mars and legendary founders of Rome) is an image of fierce maternal care that reappears in the folklore of India. It may account for the diverse stories of wolves as ancestors – of Genghis Khan for one. Turkic wolf symbolism is positive enough to suggest that it was a totemic animal in central Asia. In North America it was a dancer symbol associated with the guidance of spirits.

Greek myths of the dismaying three-headed Cerberus guarding the entrance to Hades draw on the dog's ancient links with the underworld.

Small Mammals and Amphibians

HARES and **RABBITS** have strong lunar symbolism, possibly because the moon's patches resembled leaping hares to the ancients. As a result, they were linked with menstruation and with fertility in African, Native American, Celtic, Buddhist, Chinese, Egyptian, Greek, Hindu and Teutonic tradition. The hare was an attribute of lunar and hunter goddesses in the classical and Celtic worlds, and also of the Greek gods Eros (as passion) and Hermes (as speedy messenger). Ancient associations with fertility and regeneration in Teutonic and Nordic traditions underlie the symbolism of the Easter Bunny. For its links with divinities, the hare was sometimes a forbidden food. Because of their prolific breeding, rabbits were often used in sympathetic magic as cures for sterility or difficult labour. The folk belief that a foot of the agile rabbit or hare is good for gout or rheumatism is a similar example of such occult symbolism. Folklore attributes harmless guile to rabbits, and in North American myths the lunar hare plays a creative role in shaping nature to human advantage.

The hare (illustrated here in a 14th-century Arabic book) is a semi-divine creature for some Shi'ites, linked with the Prophet's son-in-law.

Another mammal associated with fecundity is the **RAT**, more generally a symbol of destructiveness and avarice. As nocturnal raiders of granaries, rats were perceived to be harmful in the ancient Middle East, and were therefore linked with the underworld and, in Christianity, with the Devil. But a different symbolism based on their knowingness and breadwinning abilities is evident not only in folklore (their legendary foreknowledge of doomed ships) but also in their association with Asian gods of wisdom, success or prosperity. A rat is paradoxically the steed of the elephant-headed god Ganesha in Indian myth, and the companion of the Japanese god of wealth Daikoku. In the mythology of southern China, a rat brought rice to humankind. The rat is the first sign of the Chinese zodiac. Some Renaissance paintings show a black and white rat, representing night and day, gnawing at time.

MICE were associated more with timidity – an ancient symbolism, judging from the legendary insult of the Egyptian king Tachos, disappointed by the puny appearance of a Spartan ally: "The mountain laboured, Jupiter stood aghast, and a mouse ran out." In folk superstition, mice were souls that had

The open-jaws of the bat in this Mayan design depict its symbolic role as the underworld devourer of light.

slipped from the mouths of the dead (red if good, black if corrupted) – rather as doves were said to fly from the mouths of saints as their souls departed. Mice were used for divination in Africa because they were believed to understand the mysteries of the underworld.

The **BAT** was an animal of fear and superstition, often associated with death, night and, in Judeo-Christian tradition, idolatry or Satanism. Bats can also signify madness, as in Goya's nightmarish 19th century painting *The Sleep of Reason*. The bat is an underworld divinity in Central American and Brazilian mythology. It was erroneously credited with sharp eyesight both in Africa and in ancient Greece, where it symbolized perspicuity.

FROG AND TOAD

The **FROG** is a foetal symbol, most specifically in Egypt, where Heket was the frog goddess of birth. It is associated with the primeval state of matter, magic, germination, evolution, lunar phases, water and rain. Its amphibious transformation from egg and tadpole to a land-going creature with rudimentary human features, helps to explain the Grimm fairy tale of the frog who turned into a prince.

As harbingers of spring rain and regrowth, frogs also symbolized fecundity and resurrection, particularly in ancient Egypt and Asia. Frog images were good luck emblems in Japan, especially for voyagers.

In European superstition, the **TOAD** was an attribute of death and was often shown in art with a skull or skeleton, or eating the genitals of a naked woman as a symbol of lust. The toad was a loathsome familiar of witches, suggestive of the torments of the damned – a demonic symbolism that stems from the ancient Near East, based perhaps on the toad's toxic secretions. These were used medicinally in China where the toad was a lunar, yin and humid symbol, a rain-bringer, and therefore associated with luck and riches.

In folklore, a three-legged toad lived in the moon: it was said that a lunar eclipse was the act of the toad's swallowing the moon. Rain and fertility symbolism appear in Mexico and in parts of Africa where the toad is sometimes given the status of a culture hero. Alchemy associated the toad with the primal elements of earth and water.

The water symbolism of frogs led to their use in ancient China to invoke rain by sympathetic magic. The frog emblem in this Navajo sand painting suggests a similar purpose.

Creatures of the Sea

Dolphins were ancient symbols of sea power in the Mediterranean, as on this 6th century BC Etruscan vase, where they accompany a sea god.

The **FISH**, a phallic symbol of sexual happiness and fecundity, is also famous as the earliest emblem of Christ. The letters of the Greek word for "fish", *ichthus*, form an acronym for "Jesus Christ, Son of God, Saviour" (*Iesous Christos Theou hUios Soter*). Seals and lamps in the catacombs of Rome bore this emblem as a secret sign. Gospel texts reinforced its symbolism through an analogy made by Christ between fishing and converting people. Hence the "fisherman's ring" worn by the pope. The baptismal font was in Latin called *piscina* ("the fishpond"), and Christian converts were *pisciculi* ("little fishes"). Fish shown in paintings of the Last Supper are a sacramental link with the Catholic custom of eating fish instead of other meat on Fridays. Three fishes intertwined or three fishes sharing a single head are symbols of the Trinity. Hebrew tradition prepared the way for this extensive symbolism. Fishes represented the true and faithful and were the food of the Sabbath and of paradise. Priests of the ancient cult of Ea, the Mesopotamian god of the waters and wisdom, also attached sacramental meaning to fish. As creatures of boundless liberty, not threatened by the Flood, they appear as saviours in Indian myth, avatars of Vishnu and Varuna. On the soles of the Buddha's feet they symbolize freedom from the restraints of worldly desires. The Buddha and the Greek Orpheus are each called "fisher of men".

Three entwined fishes, representing the Trinity, from a stained-glass window in Wrexham priory, England.

The sexual symbolism of fish is almost universal – linked with their prolific spawn, the fertility symbolism of water, and analogies of the fish with the penis. They are associated with lunar and mother goddesses and birth. In China they are emblems of plenty and good luck.

Among individual fish, the **SALMON** acquired the specific symbolism of virility, fecundity, courage, wisdom and foresight. To coastal peoples of northern Europe and of the American northwest, salmon battling their way upstream became totemic images of nature's bounty and wisdom. For the Celts, transformation and phallic symbolism mingle in the story of Tuan mac Cairill who, in salmon form, was said to have impregnated an Irish queen to whom he was served after being caught. The Irish hero Finn scalded his thumb as he cooked the Salmon of Knowledge. He sucked his thumb to ease the pain, and in tasting the salmon's juice acquired powers of prophecy and wisdom. In China, the **CARP** is an emblem of longevity, virility and

scholastic success. It was a samurai emblem in Japan – possibly because of the contrast between its leaping vigour in the water and its calmness when hooked and dying. As symbols of good luck, images of carp were placed on ships' masts, or roofs to ward off fire.

Among aquatic mammals, the **DOLPHIN** is a widespread symbol of salvation, transformation and love – an emblem of Christ as saviour. Its symbolism is drawn directly from the nature of this friendly, playful and intelligent marine mammal. Greek, Cretan and Etruscan mythology, in which the dolphin carries gods, saves heroes from drowning, or carries souls to the Islands of the Blessed, influenced its Christian symbolism. It was an attribute of the Greek deities Poseidon (in Roman myth, Neptune), Aphrodite (Venus), Eros (Cupid), Demeter (Ceres) and Dionysus (Bacchus). As an emblem of the sacrificial Christ, the dolphin can appear pierced by a trident or with the secret cross symbol of an anchor. Entwining an anchor, the dolphin may be a symbol of prudence (speed restrained).

THE WHALE AND REBIRTH

An impressive image of the colossal in nature, the whale is also an ark or womb symbol of regeneration. Some scholars have seen the story of Jonah and the whale as an allegory of the Babylonian captivity and deliverance of the Jews. More plausibly, the belly of the whale represents the obscurity of initiation leading to a newly clarified state of life.

In Matthew's gospel, Christ draws a parallel between Jonah's experience and his own impending descent into the earth and resurrection. Jonah's burial period of three days and three nights suggests the lunar symbolism of the "dark of the moon" followed by its reappearance as a new crescent.

The whale is linked with the idea of initiation in Africa and Polynesia. Numerous myths of spiritual heroes delivered by whales also appear in southeast Asia. The whale is often linked with the aquatic monster Leviathan. Medieval images of a whale's mouth as the gate of hell were based on fanciful similes in ignorant bestiaries of the day.

The rebirth symbolism of the whale is depicted in the 12th-century Verdun altarpiece as the biblical "great fish" regurgitates the prophet Jonah.

Creatures of the Sky

Prehistoric and Egyptian paintings of **BIRD-HEADED PEOPLE** symbolize the spiritual side of human nature and, by implication, the promise of immortality. The concept of **BIRDS** as souls is as widespread as the belief that they represent goodness and joy – symbolism suggested by their lightness and rapidity, the soaring freedom of their flight, and their mediation between earth and sky. Shamans equipped with feathers and bird masks were thought to be able to fly to higher realms of knowledge. Birds thus traditionally stood for wisdom, intelligence and the swift power of thought – meanings far from the modern pejorative "bird-brained". Roman divination by the flight or song patterns of birds was perhaps an attempt to decode their superior knowledge. Birds confide useful secrets to the heroes of many fairy stories. Alternatively, as many Aboriginal tales suggest, they can bear information to their enemies. The expression, "A little bird told me," thus echoes ancient ideas. In Western art, birds can symbolize both Air and Touch.

FEATHERS themselves have ascension symbolism and are widely held as emblems of prayer. In North America, eagle-feathered headdresses associated chiefs with the Great Spirit and with the power of air, wind and thunder gods.

Among the most iconic of individual birds is the **DOVE**, whose universal importance as a peace symbol owes less to its nature (often quarrelsome) than to its beauty and the influence of biblical references. The small, white bird that returned to Noah with an olive leaf plucked from the floodwaters had irresistible charm as the image of a wrathful God making peace with humanity. The dove became a pre-Christian embodiment of the divine spirit and was seen by John the Baptist descending upon Christ after his baptism. The dove thus personifies the Holy Ghost and is a symbol of baptism. By extension the dove

The dove represents the Holy Spirit in many Annunciation scenes, in depictions of the baptism of Christ, and also in paintings of the Trinity, such as Cranach the Elder's, shown here.

represented the purified soul, and is often shown flying from the mouths of martyred saints. The dove also appears as a Christian emblem of chastity. However, it was the attribute of great Semitic and Greco-Roman love goddesses. The **PARTRIDGE** also symbolized love and feminine beauty in both Greek and Indo-Iranian tradition.

The **PHEASANT** was an emblematic bird in China, associated by its beauty and colour with the sun, light, virtue and the organizing ability of high-ranking civil servants. The Chinese also linked it with thunder, presumably from its clapping wings.

Another bird associated with light in China was the **QUAIL**, a symbol more widely of warmth, ardour and courage. In Greek and Hindu tradition, the quail symbolized the renewal of life and the return of the sun in spring.

THE REGAL PEACOCK

The tail display of the male peacock associated it with the radiance of the sun, with royalty, and with immortality. In Iranian legend, the peacock was said to kill snakes and use their saliva to create the iridescent bronze-greens and blue-gold "eyes" of its tail feathers. As the fame of the bird spread and it was put on show in the Mediterranean world, it became an emblem not only of rebirth but also of the starry firmament, and therefore of cosmic unity.

In Rome, the peacock was the soul-bird of the empress and her princesses, as the eagle was of the emperor. The Persian court was the "Peacock Throne", and peacocks are also associated with the thrones of the Hindu god Indra, and the Buddhist Amitabha, who presides over the Chinese paradise. Cherubim are borne on peacock wings, and the birds sometimes appear in Christian art at the Nativity or drinking from a chalice – both motifs of eternal life. However, Christian doctrines of humility led to an analogy between the peacock and the sins of pride, which it symbolizes in Western art. Most other traditions saw it as a wholly positive symbol of dignity, especially in China where it was the Ming dynasty emblem. Peacock dances of southeast Asia draw on the original idea of the bird as a solar emblem, its enacted "death" bringing rain.

Peacocks are the mounts or escorts of several Hindu deities, including Krishna, who is shown with them in this 18th-century Indian miniature charming cow-herd girls (Gopis) with his flute.

Birds of Prey

As master of the air, the **EAGLE** is one of the most unambiguous and universal of all symbols, embodying as it does the power, speed and perception of the animal world at its zenith. It is not only an attribute of the greatest gods but frequently a direct personification of them. As soul emblems, eagles were released from the pyres of Roman emperors. The Hebrew idea that the eagle could burn its wings in the solar fire and plummet into the ocean to emerge with a new pair (Psalm 103:5) became a motif of Christian baptismal symbolism. The eagle appears not only on fonts but on church lecterns – as the attribute of St John

The wrath of Zeus is embodied by the eagle that tears at the liver of Prometheus, stealer of fire for humankind.

SOARING EMBLEM OF THE SUN

Like the eagle, the **FALCON** is a solar emblem of victory, superiority, aspiration, spirit, light and liberty. As a hawk-like species (but with longer wings and a higher range) the falcon is hard to distinguish from the hawk in iconography, making their symbolism virtually identical. Many Egyptian gods are shown with the body or head of a falcon, including Ra, who often appears in art with a solar disk in place of the crest. Horus, god of the sky and of the day, is a falcon god. His painted hawk-like eye is a common emblem on Egyptian amulets signifying the sharpness of his protective vision. The Ba, a symbol of the individual spirit, has a hawk body and a human head. In Western tradition, the falcon is an emblem of the huntsman and is associated with the Germanic sky gods Woden and Frigg, as well as the Nordic trickster Loki.

A **HOODED FALCON** is sometimes depicted in Western art as an emblem of hope – that it will be unhooded and released to light and freedom. Predatory symbolism appears more rarely. In Peruvian art, the falcon appears with solar significance as a companion or brother soul of the Incas, and also as a human ancestor.

The falcon, or hawk, was the king of birds in ancient Egypt, an image of cosmic wholeness and of the rising sun.

the Evangelist, bearer of the Christian message. In many traditions, an eagle holding a snake in its mouth symbolizes the conquest of evil. The bird had celestial and solar symbolism in America also, and was a shamanic father symbol among nomads, particularly in northern Asia.

An ancient emblem of victory, the eagle was carried on Roman standards as "the bird of Jove". The Hittites used a double-headed eagle device, apparently still in use among the Seljuk Turks at the time of the Crusades and taken back to Europe to become the emblem of the Holy Roman Empire and later of the Austrian and Russian empires. Heraldic use of the eagle was widespread in Poland, Germany and Napoleonic France. The white-headed American eagle with outstretched wings is the emblem of the USA. In art, the eagle can be an attribute of Pride.

Among other birds of prey, the **VULTURE** is now a metaphor for opportunistic greed, but was a protective symbol in ancient Egypt. The **CROW** was a more negative symbol in Europe, where it is a carrion species. It became an emblem of war, death, solitude, evil and bad luck – a symbolism that appears in India also. The American species, which is gregarious and feeds mainly on grain and insects, has strikingly different symbolism – positive, even heroic, as in Tlingit myths where it appears as a solar, creative and civilizing bird. Both American and Aboriginal myths explain the crow's black plumage as a mishap and read no ill-omen into it. More widely, the crow appears as a guide or prophetic voice. In China, a three-legged crow on a sun disk was the imperial emblem. It also stood for filial or family love in Japan.

The **RAVEN**, too, symbolized death, loss and war in western Europe but was widely venerated elsewhere. Its Western reputation was influenced by its association as a soothsayer with Celtic battle goddesses such as the Morrigan and Badb and with the ferocious Vikings. Further east, the raven is a solar and oracular symbol, the emblem of China's Chou dynasty. It was the messenger bird of Apollo as well as of the goddess Athene in Greece, and was linked with the sun cult of Mithras. The raven appears in Africa and elsewhere as a guide, warning of dangers, and in Native North America as a culture hero. For the Inuit it is Raven Father, a creator god whose killing would bring foul weather.

Hugin and Munin, raven symbols of mind and memory, accompanied the Norse god Odin, but were interpreted as predatory Viking emblems.

Water Birds

The **SWAN** has become a romantic and ambiguous symbol of masculine light and feminine beauty in Western music and ballet. Similarly, in classical myth, the swan was the attribute both of the beautiful Greek goddess Aphrodite (in Roman myth, Venus) and of Apollo as god of poetry, prophecy and music. The Greek fable that swans sing a last song of unearthly beauty as they die reinforced the swan's association with poetry and linked it also with death, as in the Finnish legend of the Swan of Tuonela in which it personifies the waters of the underworld.

The persistent theme of transformation in swan symbolism is prefigured in the myth in which the Greek god Zeus (Jupiter) disguised himself as a swan to ravish Leda, wife of Tyndareus, the king of Sparta. Through such myths the swan evolved into a symbol of achieved passion and the ebbing or loss of love. A pair of swans, linked by a gold or silver chain, draw the Celtic barque of the sun.

The ancients were also impressed by the beauty and stamina of the **CRANE**, its migrations and spring reappearances, its complex mating dance, its voice and its contemplative stance at rest. The bird was linked in China with immortality, in Africa with the gift of speech, and widely with the ability to communicate with the gods. Its cyclic return also suggested regeneration, a resurrection symbolism sometimes used in Christianity. It personifies Vigilance in Western art. In Egypt, the double-headed crane represented prosperity.

The **STORK** was a popular emblem of longevity and, in Taoism, of immortality. There and elsewhere, storks symbolize filial devotion because they were thought to feed their elderly parents. Its nursing care and association with new life as a migratory bird of spring made it sacred to the Greek goddess Hera as a protective divinity of nursing mothers – the basis of the Western fable that storks bring babies. Christian symbolism links the stork with purity, piety and resurrection.

In Egypt, the **IBIS** was a sacred emblem of wisdom, an incarnation of the lunar

The crane (embroidered among flowers on an 18th-century Chinese surcoat) is an emblem of happiness. It could also symbolize honour and literary elegance.

deity Thoth, patron god of scribes and lord of occult knowledge. It was mummified in royal tombs to provide instruction in the mysteries of the afterlife. The mythical Egyptian Benu bird, revered as the creator of life, was based on the **HERON** emblem of the morning sun – also an ascensional image in China.

In Christianity, an elaborate symbolism was attached to the **PELICAN**. Based on the legend that these improbable-looking birds tear their breasts (rather than empty their bills) to feed their young, it became an emblem of self-sacrificial love. The earliest Christian bestiary drew an analogy between the male pelican reviving its young with blood from its pierced breast and Christ shedding his blood for humankind. The pelican sometimes appears in Crucifixion paintings with this meaning. It represents Christ's human nature when paired with the phoenix.

The pelican symbolizes filial devotion and the chief Pauline virtue, Charity, in Western still-life painting.

THE FLIGHT OF THE GOOSE

The goose has a wide range of symbolism including vigilance, loquaciousness, love, and fidelity. Its spectacular migrations also made it an emblem of freedom, aspiration and seasonal regeneration. The solar and beneficent symbolism of the wild goose is close to the swan's, and the two are interchangeable in the Celtic world. The goose was a warlike talisman both for the Celts and (as the escort of Mars) in Rome. There, it became a celebrated emblem of vigilance after an incident in 390BC when the honking of sacred geese at the temple of Juno alerted defenders of the Capitoline Hill to an attack by the Gauls. The Greeks linked the goose with Hera, Apollo, Eros, and with the messenger god Hermes. It was messenger to the gods in Egypt, too, as well as being the legendary bird that laid the cosmic egg. It became an emblem of the soul of the pharaohs (as representatives of the sun, born from the primal egg). At the accession of a new pharaoh, four geese were despatched as heralds to the cardinal points. Goose sacrifices at the December solstice symbolized the returning sun. The wild goose was the mount of Asiatic shamans, and of Brahma in India, as the soul's yearning for release from the ceaseless round of existence. A secondary symbolic theme, widespread in fable and folklore, is based on the domestic goose, going back to its association with the Sumerian goddess of the farmyard, Bau. Here its image is of a gossipy, mothering creature, sometimes foolish (the "silly goose" of idiom).

This fresco painted 4,500 years ago in the pyramid of Meidum, may refer to the solar rebirth symbolism of the goose in Egyptian ceremonies.

The Plant Kingdom

From the earliest times, plants have provided human beings not only with sustenance but also with consoling images of divine benevolence and the seasonal continuity of life. Plant symbolism is overwhelmingly positive for this reason. Dichotomy appears only in the sharp contrast between tamed and untamed nature. In the folklore and fairy tales of settled communities, the forest was a place of mysteries, dangers, trials or initiation. Being lost in the forest, or finding one's way through, is a powerful metaphor for the terrors of inexperience and the achievement of knowledge – of the adult world or of the self. Understanding the forest was a mark of shamanistic gifts, notably in Central America. At the other end of the spectrum, the garden became a symbol of paradise – notably in the arid landscapes of Egypt and Persia – because it provided a foretaste of the joys of immortality. The sealed fruitfulness of the enclosed garden became a Christian symbol of the Virgin Mary, often depicted in a garden setting.

Harmony and cosmic order are represented by the solar and lunar trees of the alchemical image above, and by the Master of Oberrheinischer's painting The Garden of Paradise *(right). Gardens symbolize the visible blessings of God (the divine gardener) and the ability of humans themselves to achieve a state of grace.*

The Tree of Life

TREES are the supreme natural symbols of dynamic growth, seasonal death and regeneration. Reverence for their power goes back to primitive beliefs that gods and spirits inhabited them. Animist symbolism of this kind survives in European folklore of the tree-man or Green Man. In fairy tales, trees can either be protective and grant wishes, or appear as frightening, obstructive, even demonic.

As mythologies developed, the idea of a tree forming a central axis for the flow of divine energy linking supernatural and natural worlds took symbolic shape in the legendary **TREE OF LIFE** – a cosmic tree, rooted in the waters of the underworld and passing through earth to heaven. An almost universal symbol, the Tree of Life often becomes a metaphor for the whole of creation. In many traditions it grows on a sacred mountain or in paradise. A fountain of spiritual nourishment may gush from its roots. A snake coiled at its base can represent spiralling energy drawn from the earth; alternatively, the serpent is a destructive symbol. Birds nest in the upper branches, emblems of celestial messengers or souls. Through the Tree of Life,

---

CHRISTMAS TREE AND YULE LOG

The Christmas tree is an emblem of rebirth, more particularly the rebirth of light – a solar symbolism dating back at least to the Roman festival of Saturnalia, when evergreen decorations celebrated the death of the old year and birth of the new.

North European yuletide rites in which fir trees were hung with lights and surrounded with sacrificial offerings are more direct antecedents of the modern decorated tree. The yule log was the centrepiece of these twelve-day Teutonic and Celtic festivities in which the ritual burning of a sacred oak branch symbolized the returning warmth and light of the sun at the December solstice. Orbs, stars and crescents hung on the fir tree originally had cosmic significance.

Both the Victorian Christmas tree and its colourful decorations were based largely on German and Austrian traditions, as in this display of children's toys from Stuttgart, Germany.

humanity ascends from its lower nature toward spiritual illumination, salvation or release from the cycle of being.

By its very form, the tree is a metaphor for evolution, its branches representing diversity, its trunk unity. In Indian iconography, a tree sprouting from the cosmic egg represents Brahma creating the manifest world. Alternatively, the **COSMIC TREE** is reversed to show its roots drawing spiritual strength from the sky and spreading it outward and downward – a favourite image in Cabbalism and other forms of mysticism.

Many **FOOD-BEARING TREES** appear as Trees of Life – the peach in China, sycamore fig in Egypt, almond in Iran, olive, palm or pomegranate in other Middle-Eastern or Semitic traditions. Their cosmic symbolism seems to have developed out of simpler cults in which the trees were embodiments of the fecund Earth Mother. Fertility rites were usually centred upon deciduous trees, whose bare winter branches and spring flowering provided apt symbols of the seasonal cycles of death and regeneration. A notable exception was the worship of Attis in Asia Minor and the Greco-Roman world. The emblematic tree of Attis was a **PINE**, a leading symbol of immortality. His death (by emasculation) and rebirth were celebrated by stripping the pine and winding it in wool – the probable origin of the maypole tradition, a tree-based fertility rite.

PAIRED TREES or trees with divided trunks often symbolize the principle of duality. In the dualist symbolism of the Near East, the Tree of Life is paralleled by a Tree of Death. This is the biblical Tree of the Knowledge of Good and Evil, whose forbidden fruit, when tasted by Eve in the Garden of Eden, brought the curse of mortality upon humankind.

This richly decorated pottery candelabrum from Mexico takes the form of a Tree of Life with devils and other figures in regional costume displaying bread and fruit at their feet.

BRANCHES, used for example in spring fertility rites, took on the symbolism of the trees from which they were cut. Thus, brandished branches of palm or olive were triumphal emblems in processions, and mistletoe branches were widespread symbols of resurrection, particularly in the Celtic world. **WOOD** itself has long had protective symbolism, probably based on ancient cults of beneficial tree spirits and on traditions in which the tree is an expression of maternal nourishment. In Indian tradition, wood is the primal substance shaping all things – Brahma.

Trees of Legend

In Oriental symbolism, the **PINE** is the most important of all resinous evergreens, representing immortality or longevity. Like the cedar, it was linked with incorruptibility and was planted around Chinese graves with this symbolism. Its resin was fabled to produce the mushrooms on which the Taoist immortals fed. The Scots pine is a favourite motif in Chinese and Japanese art, either singly representing longevity or in pairs representing married fidelity. It appears often with other emblems of longevity or renewal including the plum, bamboo, mushroom, stork and white stag. The pine is also an emblem of courage, resolution and good luck – the tree of the Shinto New Year. In the West, it was linked to agricultural fertility, particularly in the Roman spring

THE LAUREL OF APOLLO

The aromatic bay species of laurel was the crowning emblem of the Greco-Roman world for both warriors and poets through its association with Apollo. He is said to have purified himself with it in the groves of Tempe in Thessaly. Priestesses of Apollo's Delphic cult chewed laurel before giving their prophecies. It became an emblem of victory, peace, purification, divination and immortality. Laurel was also thought to deter lightning, a superstition believed by the Roman Emperor Tiberius who used to reach for his laurel wreath during thunderstorms. Associated with many deities including Dionysus (Bacchus), Zeus (Jupiter), Hera (Juno) and Artemis (Diana), laurel was an emblem of truce as well as triumph. A secondary symbolism of chastity derives from the myth that the nymph Daphne was turned into a laurel as she fled Apollo's lust. Laurel had talismanic significance in North Africa; in China it appears as the tree beneath which the lunar hare mixes the elixir of immortality.

The winged figure of Victory wears a wreath of laurel in an Ingres study for his painting of the Apotheosis of Homer.

rebirth rites of Cybele and Attis. The pine was sacred also to the Greek god Zeus (Jupiter in Roman myth). The pine cone itself is a phallic and flame symbol of masculine generative force. Surmounting a column (sometimes mistaken for the pineapple), it was an emblem of Marduk – the Mesopotamian hero god.

A more enigmatic evergreen is the **CYPRESS**, a Western symbol of death and mourning, but in Asia and elsewhere an emblem of longevity, endurance and even immortality (it was the Phoenician Tree of Life). In Sumeria, the Tree of Life was the **CEDAR**, a symbol of power and immortality. Its reputation for longevity may account for the use of cedar resin by Celtic embalmers. The beneficial, protective tree of northern European and Asian peoples was the **BIRCH**, sacred to the greatest Germanic gods and the emblem of Estonia. It was the Cosmic Tree of Central Asia. Nomads used birch for the centre pole of their yurts (tents), and it had sacred meaning in shamanistic rites as a symbol of human ascent to the spirit world. Its supposed ability to deflect evil may explain why witches were birched to rid them of demons.

The acacia emblem on this Masonic regalia is an initiation symbol. The Hebrew Tabernacle was of acacia, and in legend a branch covered the grave of Solomon's master-builder.

The **OAK** has ancient links with nobility and endurance. It may have been sacred to the thunder gods of Greece, Germany and the ancient Celtic peoples because it was thought to bear the brunt of lightning strikes. In Druidic rites, it served as an axial symbol and natural temple, associated with male potency and wisdom. Although mainly a male emblem, the oak is linked with mythical women – Cybele, Juno and other Great Mother Goddesses, as well as the Dryads, the oak nymphs.

As a lunar and feminine symbol, the **WILLOW** is one of the most celebrated of all motifs in Chinese art and decoration. It was a Taoist metaphor for patience and strength in flexibility. In Tibetan tradition, it is the Tree of Life. In Japan the Ainu said it was the backbone of the first man. Painkillers extracted from its bark may account for its association with health, easy childbirth and other medical and magical benefits in both Asian and Western traditions. Still greater powers were attributed to the **HAZEL**, a tree associated with divination, wisdom, fertility and rain. In northern Europe and the Celtic world, the hazel wand was the instrument of wizards and fairies, diviners and seekers of gold. It was thought to bring luck to lovers, and according to Norman folklore, drew abundant milk from cows struck with a hazel ring.

The long-lived ginkgo is a celebrated tree in Asia where it is an emblem of immortality in China and of loyalty in Japan. It was said to be willing to die for its owner.

Trees of Plenty

Given its importance as a food source in the ancient world, it is not surprising to find the **FIG** appearing as the sacred tree of life in many regions (notably in Egypt, India, southeast Asia and parts of Oceania). Graphic links between the fig leaf and the male genitals, together with the milky juice extracted from larger varieties of fig trees as a form of rubber, added powerful sexual aspects to its symbolism. The fig leaf convention in art goes back to the biblical story of Adam and Eve using fig leaves to protect their modesty when they ate the forbidden fruit and "knew that they were naked" (Genesis 3:7). For the Greeks the fig was an attribute of Priapus as well as Dionysus. In Roman tradition, the infants Romulus and Remus, were suckled under the protective shade of a fig, which hence became an augury of national prosperity, a symbolism found in Judaism, too. The fig had fecundity symbolism both in Egypt and in India where it was linked with the procreative power of Vishnu and Shiva, and where the sacred Bo variety was the tree beneath which the Buddha achieved spiritual enlightenment. Hence its significance in Buddhism as an emblem of moral teaching and of immortality.

Like the fig, the **OLIVE** appears in Islamic tradition as the forbidden fruit tree in paradise. A blessed tree in Judeo-Christian and classical symbolism, it is most famously associated with peace. But it can also symbolize victory, joy, plenty, purity, immortality and virginity.

As an early, important and exceptionally durable crop in the Mediterranean world, the olive was sacred in Greece to the warlike goddess Athene, who is said to have invented the tree for Athens, thereby winning a contest with Poseidon for the patronage of the city. Brides wore or carried olive leaves (signifying virginity), and olive wreaths crowned victors at the Olympic Games (indeed, the word "Olympic" is closely related to the word "olive") . The peace symbolism of the olive became dominant under the Pax Romana when olive branches were presented by envoys submitting to the imperial power. For Jewish and Christian symbolists, the olive sprig brought back to Noah by the

The olive tree is a symbol of peace, concord and wisdom in Western art. It appears widely in Christian tradition, for example as an attribute of the archangel Gabriel and of the Virgin Mary. In Japan it is an emblem of friendship and success, in China of calmness.

dove (initially signifying nothing more than this tree's hardiness) acquired the Roman meaning of a sign of God's making peace with humankind.

The majestic **PALM** with its huge, feathery leaves was a solar and triumphal symbol in the ancient Middle East; it was equated with the Tree of Life in both Egypt and Arabia. As a food source, one species, the date palm, also had feminine, fecundity symbolism both in western Asia and China. Thus, palm motifs are associated not only with the Roman sun cult of Apollo but also with the goddesses Astarte and Ishtar. Emblematic use of palm fronds in victory processions (and as awards to winning gladiators) was adapted by Christ's followers to publicize his final entry into Jerusalem, which is now celebrated on Palm Sunday. Pilgrims who had visited the Holy Land were "palmers". Palm forms on lamps or other funerary objects symbolize resurrection.

The palm, a symbol of victory, fame or immortality, became the attribute in art of many Christian saints and martyrs.

A less familiar tree that holds great sacred significance in the desert regions of the Middle East is the **TAMARISK**. Its honey-like resin is a possible source, with lichen, of the biblical **MANNA**, which became a symbol of divine grace in Judaism. The tamarisk is still a free food of the Bedouin.

ORIENTAL MAGIC OF THE PEACH

The peach is one of the most favourable of all Chinese and Japanese symbols, its wood, blossom and fruit linked with immortality, longevity, spring, youth, marriage and protective magic. In Chinese myth, the peach Tree of Immortality, tended by the Queen of Heaven, Xi Wang Mu, fruits every 3,000 years. Peachwood was widely used to make miraculous bows, talismans, oracular figures and effigies of tutelary gods; and peach boughs were laid outside houses at New Year. Apotropaic significance appears in Japanese myth too, where the creator hero Izanagi routs eight pursuing thunder gods by hurling three peaches at them. Peach blossom is an emblem of virginity; and the peach is one of the Three Blessed Fruits of Buddhism. In Western Renaissance art, a peach with a leaf attached was an emblem of truthfulness – a reference to earlier use of this image as a symbol of the tongue speaking from the heart.

Shou Lao, Chinese god of longevity, holds a peach in this carving. The apple, pear, plum and citron can also symbolize longevity in China.

Shrubs, Herbs and Grasses

Like the hazel, the **HAWTHORN** was a shrub or small tree invested with magical properties in Europe. In classical times it was linked with Hymen, god of weddings. The flowers were used for marriage garlands, the wood for marriage torches. The association between its spring flowering and virginity led to folk superstitions that it protected chastity. The **HOLLY** is a more famous emblem of hope and joy. It was among the evergreens carried at the midwinter festival of Saturnalia in Rome, but its use at Christmas is linked more directly with Teutonic customs of decorating houses with holly in December.

Another evergreen, **MYRTLE**, was a Gnostic life symbol in Iraq. Perhaps because of its purple berries, this fragrant shrub, growing wild in the Mediterranean and sometimes used for victors' wreaths, was chiefly associated with love goddesses, especially the Greek Aphrodite, and with rituals surrounding marriage and childbirth. It was a Chinese emblem of success.

In Chinese tradition, **BAMBOO** symbolized resilience, longevity, happiness and spiritual truth; while in Japan it signified the characteristics of truthfulness and devotion. Used throughout the Orient as a calligraphic tool, its pure line and hollow stem had emblematic meaning for Buddhist and Taoist writers and artists. South American tribes used bamboo as a cutting tool, blowpipe and instrument of sacred music, and some revered tall species of bamboo as Trees of Life. In Africa bamboo also had sacred significance because it was ritually used for circumcision.

The **REED** is a Japanese emblem of purification in the creation myth of Izanagi, perhaps by association with water. "The Reed Plain" is a Japanese metaphor for the mortal world. The reed also had purification symbolism in the Celtic world and was superstitiously thought effective against witches. It had fertility symbolism in Mesoamerica. In Classical traditions it is an emblem of the god Pan (from his invention of the reed "pan pipes") and of music generally. The reed is a symbol of Christ's Passion because a sponge, soaked in

Holly, painted here by Rogier van der Weyden, is linked in Christian tradition with the Passion of Christ – a symbolism suggested by its thorny leaves and blood-red berries.

vinegar, was put on the end of a reed to reach Christ's mouth as he was crucified. It also appears as an emblem of St John the Baptist.

AMARANTH is depicted on Greek tombs and sculptures as a symbol of immortality. This long-lasting flowering plant was linked with Artemis, – the Greek goddess of childbirth and motherhood – and credited with healing properties. In China, its flowers were offered to the lunar hare at the Moon Festival as a token of immortality.

In China, bamboo, one of the three auspicious plants of winter (along with the pine and plum), had sacred significance for scholars. The title of this painting is The Seven Sages of the Bamboo Grove.

The symbolism of the **THISTLE** as the heraldic emblem of both Scotland and Lorraine is retaliation. Adam is punished with thistly ground in Genesis. However, like some other spiny plants, the thistle was associated with healing or talismanic powers and the white-spotted Lady's thistle is linked with the milk of the Virgin Mary. In art, thistles are emblems of martyrdom.

Another thorny plant, **ACANTHUS**, was a Greco-Roman triumphal image of life's trials surmounted, a symbolism suggested by the plant's thorns and its vigorous growth. Stylized acanthus leaves on the Corinthian capital may refer to a Greek myth of an acanthus springing up on the grave of a dead hero.

THE MYSTIC GOLDEN BOUGH

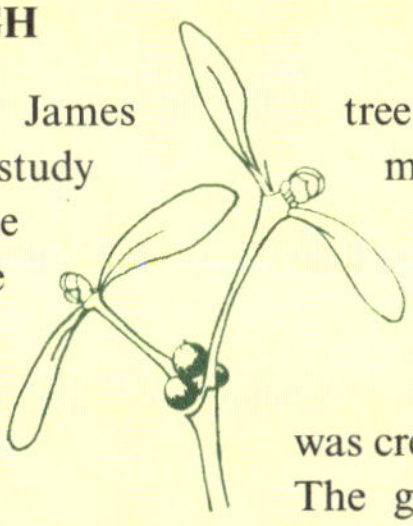

The "Golden Bough" of Sir James Frazer's provocative 19th-century study of mythology and folklore was the humble parasite **MISTLETOE**. He credited it with fire, lightning and rebirth symbolism, linking the plant with ancient sacrificial customs. As an evergreen parasite that produces yellowish flowers, and white berries in midwinter, mistletoe symbolized the continuing potency of the deciduous trees on which it was found. Mistletoe clinging to the sacred oak was a fertility and regeneration symbol to the Druids who, according to the Roman author Pliny (*c.*24–79BC), cut it with a golden sickle and sacrificed a young white bull beneath the tree – probably during midsummer and midwinter rites. The berry juice (equated with the tree's semen and its connotations of power and wisdom) supposedly prevented sterility or disease in cattle and was credited with other healing properties.

The golden bough of life becomes an instrument of death in the myth of Odin's son Balder, who is killed by a mistletoe dart. This inversion of the plant's symbolism suggests the passage from mortal to immortal status. Celtic tradition seems to account for Christmas kisses under mistletoe – an augury of fruitful union.

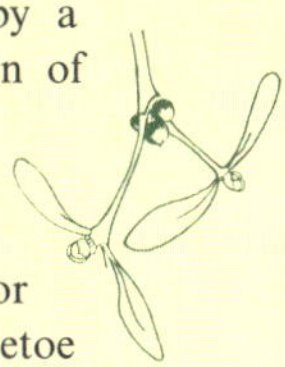

Nature's Bounty

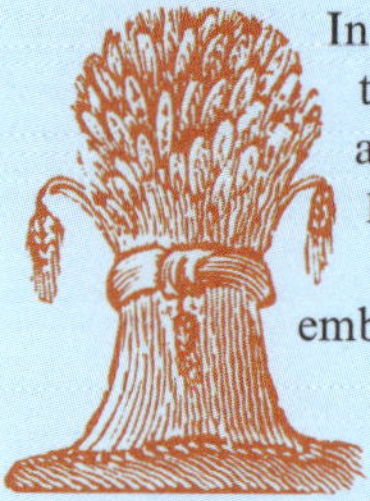

In regions where grain was the staple crop of the ancient world, **CORN**, **BARLEY**, **WHEAT** and **RICE** were central emblems of growth, rebirth and fertility. Grain ripening in the earth and reappearing in spring symbolized life after death. With this meaning, corn was a funerary emblem in China, Rome, the Middle East and Egypt, where it was specifically represented by the dying and resurrecting god Osiris. In art, ears of grain appear as attributes of most earth gods and goddesses. The Aztecs worshipped several corn gods, major and minor, while in Peru fertility was represented as a woman made of maize stalks. Blue-painted maize icons in North America symbolized the fertilizing synthesis of red earth and blue sky. Corn can also represent abundance and prosperity.

BREAD was a Christian metaphor for the food of the spirit, and for the body of Christ himself. Unleavened loaves symbolize purification and sacrifice at the Jewish Passover. In Asia, a corresponding symbolism of divine nourishment was attached to rice, used as a fecundity symbol at Indian weddings. Rice appears in mythology as the gift of a culture hero or as the food pro-

In Jan Brueghel's painting, grottoes laden with nature's bounty symbolize the paradise in which Odysseus dallied on Calypso's island.

vided for the first humans in the primeval gourd. Rice wine was drunk ritually in China as a sacred drink, and rice grains, which had protective symbolism, were placed in the mouths of the dead. In Japan, Inari was a god not only of rice but also of prosperity.

BEANS also had fecundity symbolism. They were used as love charms in India, and were popular talismans in Japan where they were customarily scattered in a house to ward off lightning and evil spirits.

Woman and bear seem drunk with pleasure as they share the divine blessings of honey in this charming scene from a 15th-century French herbal.

Among other plants used as a symbol of life arising from death was the **MUSHROOM** – an important emblem of longevity and happiness in China, and the legendary food of the immortals in Taoist tradition. Mushrooms personify souls of the reborn in some parts of central Europe, and Africa. Their magical sudden appearance, and possibly the use of some varieties as hallucinogens, may account for folklore associations with the supernatural, leading to the notion of pixie houses or witches' rings.

Major symbolism was also attached to **HONEY** – a food linked with immortals, seers and poets, and widely associated with purity, inspiration, eloquence, the divine Word and God-given blessings. Honey was the basis of mead, a sacred beverage in many cultures, equated with the nectar of the gods. Its celestial qualities seemed borne out by its golden colour. The biblical land of Canaan flowing with milk and honey was an image of spiritual as well as physical plenty. Honey was used not only as a votive food but also as an anointing, cleansing and embalming fluid in many ancient Middle-Eastern cultures.

HORN OF PLENTY

The **CORNUCOPIA**, overflowing with fruits, flowers and grains, is a symbol in Western art not only of abundance and prosperity but also of divine generosity. Ancient associations between the horn and fertility lie behind the classical story that Zeus (in Roman myth, Jupiter) accidentally broke off a horn of the goat Amaltheia that suckled him, whereupon the horn provided an inexhaustible supply of food and drink. The cornucopia appears in paintings as an attribute not only of vegetation or wine divinities such as the classical Demeter (Ceres), Dionysus (Bacchus), Priapus and Flora, but also of many positive allegorical figures including earth, Autumn, Hospitality, Peace, Fortune and Concord. Putti (types of angels) were often painted spilling nourishment (for the spirit) from a cornucopia.

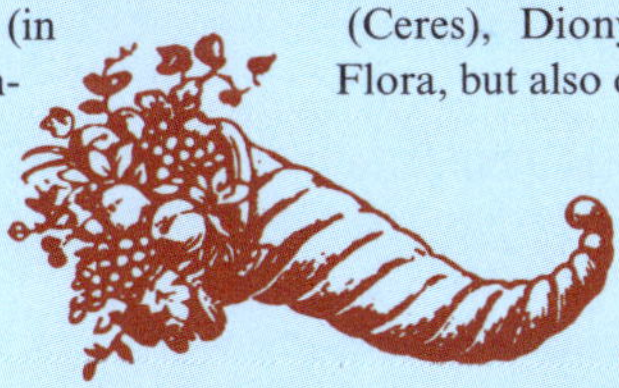

The legendary Horn of Plenty, which could not be emptied, is a feminine symbol of maternal nourishment and love.

Grapes and Wine

The **GRAPEVINE** is one of the oldest symbols of natural fecundity in the ancient Near East – and a still more important symbol of spiritual life and regeneration in both the pagan and Christian worlds. The vine was the first plant grown by Noah after the biblical Flood, and in the Book of Exodus a branch with grapes was the first sign that the Israelites had reached the Promised Land. Its symbolism of a god-given gift accounts for the continuing importance of wine in Jewish ritual. Christian symbolism is still more specific. "I am the true vine, and my Father is the vinegrower," says Christ in the Gospel of St John (15:1). The vine becomes a spiritual symbol of regeneration and in the Eucharist wine is figuratively – or in Catholic doctrine literally – transformed into Christ's blood.

WINE is a symbol of transformation because the juice of the crushed grape held the mysterious power to change itself into something more potent – and to change those who drank it. This, and the blood colour of red wine, is the basis of its sacramental symbolism. It was made in the Near East at least 5,000 years ago and was regarded as a sign of the vigour of nature and the beneficent spirit animating it. Libations of wine poured on the earth signified fertility and life after death. The cult of the Greek god Dionysus (in Roman myth, Bacchus) made wine a symbol of ecstatic union with the god himself. Christianity gave this symbolism new poetic force: "Those who eat my flesh and drink my blood abide in me and I in them" (John 6:56). Medieval paintings of Christ standing or kneeling in a wine press refer to the description of him by St Augustine (354–430) as "the bunch that has been put under the wine press"; and in some images of the crucifixion, the cross itself is transformed into a wine press, the upright post depicted with a spiral thread. Alternatively, blood streaming from pressed grapes symbolizes God's wrath, as in Revelation (14:20).

A subsidiary symbolism of wine is that it produces truth, either by "opening the heart to reason" in a Rabbinical phrase, or by loosening the tongues of liars and hypocrites. The Bible takes a fairly tolerant view of wine-bibbing as a folly. Noah is shamed rather than condemned for it. "These men are full of new wine," say mockers when the Apostles begin speaking in tongues. However, full **WINESKINS** are sometimes emblems of sin. Islam reserves wine for those who have reached paradise – for the Prophet did not condemn wine, only its abuse. In certain contexts, grapes and wine can symbolize drunken folly.

Bunches of grapes were symbols of redemption through Christ in funerary art, but have been used more widely as traditional emblems of hospitality and conviviality, celebrating the bounty of autumn.

Vinous motifs almost overwhelm Caravaggio's Young Bacchus. *Like earlier vegetation gods in Mesopotamia, Bacchus (Dionysus in Greek myth) was identified with the grape. To his Orphic cult, wine was his sacrificial blood.*

Favoured Fruits

A golden apple awarded by Paris to the fairest Greek goddess, as depicted here by Joachim Utewael, eventually led to the Trojan War after he chose the sensual Aphrodite.

The most emblematic of fruits next to the grape is the **APPLE**. It represents bliss, especially sexual – a symbolism perhaps linked with the vulva shape of the core in long-section. The apple appears almost everywhere in Europe as an emblem of love, marriage, springtime, youth, fertility and longevity or immortality. Greek, Celtic and Nordic mythology all describe it as the miraculously sustaining fruit of the gods. In the book of Genesis, the fruit that tempted Eve is unnamed. However, later interpreters of scripture identified it as the apple because it was then the most popular choice as an object of desire. It thus became an image of temptation, and in Christian art symbolizes Original Sin when it is shown in the mouth of an ape or serpent. In paintings of Christ holding or reaching for an apple, it symbolizes redemption. (The pomegranate, orange or cherry are sometimes substituted by artists.)

Because Eve plucked the apple from the Tree of the Knowledge of Good and Evil, the apple also became associated with knowledge. Hermetic science, noting the "quintessential" five-fold shape of the cross-sectioned core, attached this meaning to it. In China the apple stands for peace.

Major symbolism is also attached to the **ALMOND**. It represents not only purity but also virgin birth – a mythic association that has both pagan and biblical roots. The juice of the pressed almond was equated in the ancient world with semen, leading to the story that Attis, consort of the Phrygian and Greco-Roman earth goddess Cybele, was conceived from an almond, the pure fruit of nature. In the Bible, God's sign that Aaron should have priestly status was a rod that blossomed miraculously and produced almonds. This story shares in the virgin birth symbolism of the almond-shaped aureole (mandorla) enclosing Christ and Mary in medieval iconography.

The **PEAR** is a mother or love symbol, its erotic associations probably taken from the swelling shape of the fruit, suggesting the female pelvis or breast. Linked in classical mythology with the Greek goddesses Aphrodite and Hera, the pear was also a longevity symbol in China, because the tree itself is long-lived. More curiously, the Chinese made a non-edible fruit, the **CITRON**

one of its Three Blessed Fruits, because the "fingered" citron species was taken as the hand of the Buddha. The **LEMON**'s symbolism of bitterness, failure or disappointment is predictable, although in Christian art it can represent faithfulness.

The **CHERRY** was a samurai emblem in Japan, perhaps because the hard kernel within the blood-coloured skin and flesh suggested a poetic association with the warrior caste. In China, the cherry symbolizes virginity and was also used as a heraldic emblem signifying good fortune. The vulva is a "cherry spring". In Christian iconography the cherry is yet another alternative to the apple as the fruit of paradise. Because it bears flowers before leaves, it is also a symbol of man born naked into the world.

THE SENSUAL POMEGRANATE

The other fruit strongly identified with sexual temptation is the pomegranate. Its multicellular structure and the many seeds bedded in juicy pulp within its leathery casing also led to subsidiary emblematic meanings – the oneness of the diverse cosmos, the manifold blessings of God, and the unity of many under a single authority, secular or ecclesiastical. An ancient Persian fruit, known to the Romans as the "apple of Carthage", the pomegranate was predominantly linked with fertility, love and marriage, both in the Mediterranean world and in China, where it was one of the Three Blessed Fruits of Buddhism. In the vegetation myth that tells how Proserpina, daughter of the grain goddess, was kidnapped by Hades, he gives her a pomegranate (symbolizing indissoluble wedlock) when she seeks to return to the earth's surface. By eating it, Proserpina condemns herself to return to the underworld each winter. The fruit was said to have sprung from the blood of Dionysus (a spring fertility god).

Rossetti's painting shows Proserpina holding a bitten pomegranate. She returned from the underworld every spring to regenerate the earth.

Flowers

Flowers almost universally symbolize beauty, spring, youth and gentleness – but often also innocence, peace, spiritual perfection, the brevity of life or the joys of paradise. Essentially, the flower is a concise symbol of nature at its summit, condensing into a brief span of time the cycle of birth, life, death and rebirth. Ikebana, the Japanese art of flower arrangement, is based on this symbolic theme. Flowers have spiritual significance in many religions. Thus Brahma and the Buddha are shown emerging from flowers; the dove-like columbine is the flower of the Holy Spirit; and the Virgin Mary is depicted holding a **LILY** or **IRIS**. Flowers also appear in art as attributes of Hope and the dawn, and particularly in still-lifes as reminders of evanescence. The colours, scents and qualities of flowers often determine their symbolism – the heavily-perfumed **FRANGIPANI** of sexual invitation, for example. The funerary use of more delicately scented flowers as emblems of continuing life or rebirth is known from the ancient Middle East.

The chrysanthemum is valued throughout the Orient, as shown in this statue of a Tibetan lama surrounded by flowers symbolizing contemplation.

An imperial flower of China is the **PEONY**, associated with wealth, glory and dignity because of its showy beauty. It was a Japanese fertility symbol, linked with joy and marriage. In the West its roots, seeds and flowers had an ancient medicinal reputation, hence its name, taken from the Greek word for "healer" and from the Paeon who tended to the gods wounded at Troy. The peony is sometimes identified as the "rose without a thorn".

This Japanese emblem combines the peony with the corn among which it grows. In Japan it symbolizes joy, married happiness, and fertility.

In Japan, a **CHRYSANTHEMUM** with 16 petals is the imperial and solar emblem, linked with longevity and joy. It is a Chinese symbol of Taoist perfection, autumnal tranquillity and plenitude – perhaps because its blooms continue into winter. Another important flower in Asian symbolism is the **CAMELLIA**, a Chinese image of health and fortitude, but associated in Japan with sudden death. Among other flowers associated with death, grief or the fleeting nature of life is the **ANEMONE** – symbolism based on the ephemeral nature of this wild flower, its scarlet petals, and its name (meaning "of the wind"). Anemones are identified with the biblical "flowers of the field" and sometimes appear in crucifixion scenes. They were also linked with dying god symbolism from the Greek myth that they sprang up where Adonis fell dead.

The **PANSY** is an emblem of fond remembrance, hence its common name "heartsease". The word pansy comes from the French *pensée* ("thought"). Some symbologists have proposed a tortuous link between this and the number five, the number of petals that the flower has. The symbolism of the petals is more plausibly based on their heart-like shape and the "thoughts" of the heart.

Two flowers whose symbolism is often confused are the **MARIGOLD** and **HELIOTROPE**, both solar emblems. The marigold is linked in China with longevity, in India with Krishna, and in the West with the purity and perfection of the Virgin Mary, after whom it was named ("Marygold"). The heliotrope flower symbolizes adoration – from its habit of turning toward the sun. In Greek myth, the lovesick girl Clytie was transformed into this flower, forever following the object of her hopeless passion, the sun god Helios. The flower became a Christian emblem of religious devotion.

FLOWERS OF REMEMBRANCE

In art, the **POPPY** is commonly used as an emblem of the Greek gods of sleep (Hypnos) and dreams (Morpheus); and in allegory, of Night personified – a symbolism based on the properties of the opium poppy which grew as a wild flower in Greece and the eastern Mediterranean, and was used for herbal infusions from ancient times. The narcotic aspects of the flower explain why the poppy was linked also with the Greek agricultural goddess Demeter (Ceres in Roman myth) and her daughter Persephone (Proserpina) as a symbol of the winter "sleep"of vegetation. Christianity borrowed aspects of this older tradition, making the red poppy an emblem of Christ's sacrifice and "sleep of death". The battlefields of Flanders gave fresh poignancy to the sacrificial symbolism of the red poppy.

The common poppy is one of several red or red-spotted flowers associated with blood sacrifice and the death of gods and humans.

Lotus and Narcissus

No flower has more ancient and prolific symbolism than the **LOTUS** in the traditions of Egypt, India, China and Japan. Its unique importance is based both on the decorative beauty of its radiating petals and on an analogy between them and an idealized form of the vulva as the divine source of life. By extension, the lotus came to symbolize, among other things, birth and rebirth, as well as the origin of cosmic life, and the creator gods or the sun and sun gods. It also represented human spiritual growth from the folded bud of the heart, and the soul's potential to attain divine perfection. In Egypt, the lotus, rising from bottom mud as a water lily to unfold its immaculate petals to the sun, suggested the glory of the sun's own emergence from the primeval slime: a metaphor for creation.

The lotus is the leading symbol of the Hindu goddess Shri, consort of the deity Vishnu. Alternative names for her mean "lotus".

As a decorative funerary motif symbolizing resurrection, the lotus appeared in ancient Greece and Italy, and in western Asia where decorative Egyptian lotus forms were the origin of the Ionic order of capitals in architecture. In Hinduism the sacred lotus grew from the navel of Vishnu as he rested on the waters, giving birth to Brahma (a representation of spiritual growth). The lotus is a symbol of what is divine or immortal in humanity, and is almost a synonym of perfection. Indian iconography is full of gods or bodhisattvas sitting cross-legged in the centre of flame-like lotus petals symbolizing the realization of inner potential. A parallel concept is the "golden blossom" of Chinese Taoism, a Buddhist-inspired tradition in which the lotus is again a symbol of spiritual unfolding. The sexual imagery of the lotus, most marked in Tantric Buddhism, sometimes combines the male stem and female blossom as a symbol of spiritual union and harmony. This is the "jewel in the lotus" invoked in the mantra *Om mani padme hum*.

Chinese Buddhism, in which the lotus is one of the Eight Auspicious Signs, added further symbolic associations – rectitude, firmness, conjugal harmony and prosperity – especially the blessing of many children, represented by a boy holding a lotus. The lotus represents the Buddha himself and is an image of the spiritual flowering that leads to nirvana. Sacred and profane symbolism mix in Chinese tradition – a courtesan was known as a "golden lotus", although the lotus is more generally linked with purity, even virginity, and is a Japanese emblem of incorruptible morality. It appears also in Mayan iconography, apparently with rebirth symbolism.

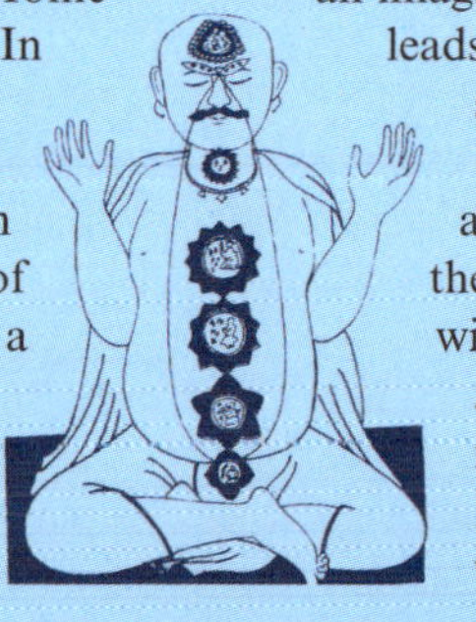

Yogic chakras chanelling energy along the body in this Indian diagram take the form of wheel-like lotuses.

SPIRIT OF THE BEAUTIFUL DEAD

The **NARCISSUS** is a flower of spring, but also a symbol of youthful death, sleep and rebirth. The wide range of plants belonging to this genus (which also include daffodils and jonquils) may account for its great variety of symbolism.

The Narcissus of classical mythology was a beautiful youth who fell in love with his own reflection in a pool and pined away gazing at it, becoming the flower that bears his name. The Roman writer Ovid developed the tale into an allegory of homosexual self-love or, in more general terms, vanity and morbid introspection. But it was based on straightforward earlier symbolism of the narcissus flower and on ancient superstitions about reflective surfaces. The narcissus flower blooms and dies early. And, as the anthropologist J. G. Frazer pointed out, self-reflections were once widely feared to be omens of death.

The narcissus was the flower that Proserpina was gathering when the chariot of Hades erupted from the earth and the king of the underworld carried her off to his realm. It was used in the rites of Proserpina's mother, the grain goddess, and planted on graves to symbolize the idea that death was only a sleep. The Greek name for the flower has the same root as "narcosis": *narké*, "numbness"). The fragrance of the narcissus flower symbolized youth in Persia. Its upright stem also made it an Islamic emblem of the faithful servant or believer. Because it bloomed at the Chinese New Year, it was a symbol of joy, good luck or a happy marriage in Oriental tradition.

The nymph with Narcissus in the painting by John William Waterhouse is Echo, whose love for him was ignored as he gazed entranced at his own image.

Lily and Rose

France's Fleur-de-lis emblem combines associations of purity with a masculine spear-like shape to denote royal power.

One of the most ambiguous of all flower symbols, the **LILY** is identified with Christian piety, purity and innocence, but was associated with fertility and erotic love in older traditions through its phallic pistil and scent. It symbolized the fertility of the Earth Goddess, and in the practice of alchemy represented the female principle.

As a favourite garden flower of antiquity, the white lily was fabled to have sprung from the milk of the Greek goddess Hera and was linked with fecundity not only in Greece but also in Egypt and the Middle East generally, where it was a popular decorative motif. Lilies symbolized prosperity and royalty in Byzantium, and these associations, rather than the link with purity, may have been the original reason for the choice of the **FLEUR-DE-LIS**, a

THE LILY IN CHRISTIAN ART

The white lily found in Christian art was, in the 19th century, named the "Madonna" lily after its association with the virginity of Mary (it is also an attribute of her husband Joseph and of her parents). The archangel Gabriel often holds a white lily in Annunciation paintings. Its emblematic significance for Christian saints is taken largely from the Sermon on the Mount in which Jesus used the glorious "lilies of the field" as an allegory of how God provided for those who renounced the pursuit of wealth. However, the white lily can sometimes also appear with opposite meanings as a portent of death or funerary emblem.

Chastity is the symbolism of the white lily in Veneziano's altar panel of the Annunciation.

stylized lily with three flowers (rather like the bearded iris), as the emblem of France.

The paragon of flowers in Western tradition is the **ROSE** – a mystic symbol of the heart, the centre of the cosmic wheel, and also of sacred, romantic and sensual love. The white rose is an emblem of innocence, purity and virginity, hence the description of the Virgin Mary as the Rose of Heaven. The red rose symbolizes passion, desire and voluptuous beauty. Both are symbols of perfection. The rose's association with eternal life caused rose petals to be scattered on graves at the Roman festival of Rosaria, and Roman emperors wore rose wreaths as crowns. Mortality is symbolized by the blown rose, and the red rose can signify spilt blood, martyrdom, death and resurrection. Roman myth linked the red rose, through its colour, with the war-god Mars and his consort Venus, and with her slain lover Adonis.

The rose was also an emblem of the sun and dawn and was linked with the Greek deity Dionysus, as well as the goddess Hecate, the Graces and the Muses.

In Christianity, the blood-red rose with its thorns was a poignant symbol of the love and suffering of Christ. For this reason, and for its more ancient associations, the rose became the focal image of the Cabbalistic Rosicrucian society, its multilayered petals representing stages of initiation into secret knowledge. The rosette (the rose seen from above) and the Gothic rose also have wheel symbolism, connoting the unfolding of generative power – making the rose a Western equivalent of the emblematic Asian lotus. In the related symbolism of Freemasonry, three St John's roses represent light, love and life. An important secondary meaning of the rose is discretion. In a Roman myth, Cupid stops rumours about Venus' infidelities by bribing the god of silence with a rose. With this meaning, roses were hung or painted above Roman council tables as signs that conversation was *sub rosa* – private, not public.

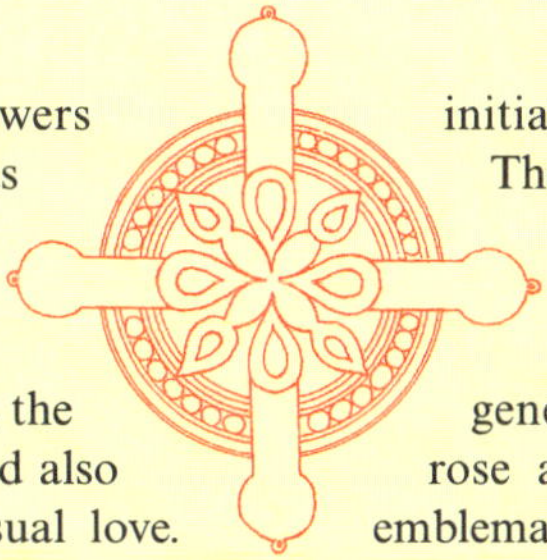

The occult 17th-century Rosicrucian society added cross and wheel symbolism to its emblem with a rose at its heart.

White roses, proffered by the woman in this 15th-century herbal manuscript, symbolize the cup of eternal life – their Roman meaning.

Spirits of the Cosmos

The Greek word *kosmos* denotes an ordered universe. To the ancients, the imposition of order upon a primeval chaos of vast scale was inconceivable without the existence of gods or other supernatural beings. The seemingly unpredictable destructive power of natural forces implied also a continous struggle for control in which cooperation between human beings and divine spirits appeared to be crucial to survival. For these reasons, cosmic symbolism was essentially religious. Early science sought to create symbolic correspondences between four primary constituents of the universe – the elements of water, air, fire and earth. Greek philosophers added a fifth – ether – representing quintessential spirit. Achieving a balance between the elements was viewed as the basis of cosmic harmony. Air and fire were seen as active and masculine, water and earth as passive and feminine. Increasingly arbitrary correspondences including colours and stages of life were added in an attempt to construct a coherent symbolic system, which collapsed only with the arrival of modern science.

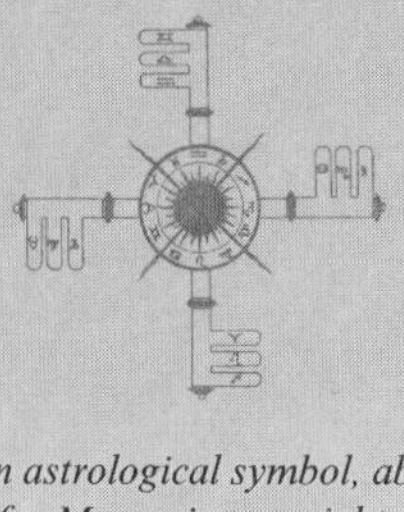

The balanced Egyptian astrological symbol, above, contrasts with the precarious mood of a Mayan image, right. A turtle representing the constellation Orion is suspended on cords from a skyband below which two solar eclipse symbols are omens of cosmic danger.

The Celestial Sphere

The **SKY** is universally associated with supernatural forces and symbolizes dominion, spiritual ascension and aspiration. Ritual canopies held above leaders in Asia and elsewhere are sky symbols of royalty or governance. The fertilizing influence of sun and rain, the eternal presence of the stars, the tidal pull of the moon and the destructive forces of storms all helped to establish the sky as the source of cosmic power.

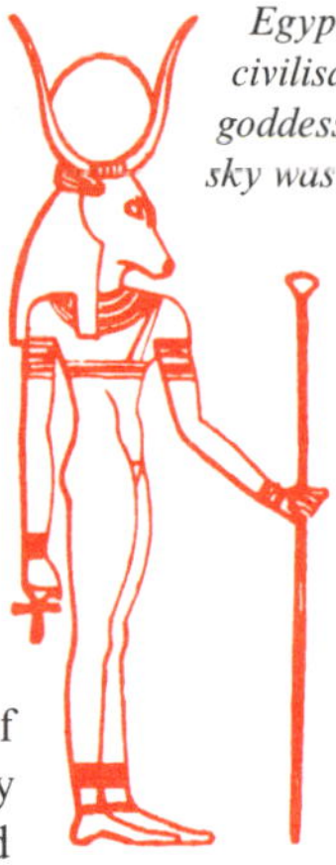

Egypt was one of the few major civilisations to personify the sky as a goddess, as in this image of Hathor. The sky was usually a masculine or yang symbol.

STARS were particular symbols of guidance and guardianship. The early belief that they ruled or influenced human life, either as divinities or as agents of divinity, underlies the hugely influential symbol system of astrology. In religion, stars formed the crowns of several great fertility goddesses, notably Ishtar in the Near East, and the Virgin Mary. Stars often symbolized cosmic windows or points of entry to heaven. They could also represent divine eyes – particularly those of Mithras, the Persian god of light. In the Old Testament, the "star out of Jacob" is a Messianic symbol, recalled in the New Testament description of Christ as "the bright and morning star". **METEORITES** were thought to be fragments of the governing stars – angels in material form, recalling humans to the existence of a higher life. Meteoric stone or metal thus had sacred value in the ancient world. The Kaaba, focal point of Mecca, contains a meteorite.

In general symbolism, the most significant stars are the **POLE STAR** and the "star" of **VENUS** – the aggressively bright emblem of warfare and life-energy as the morning star, and of sexual pleasure and fertility as the evening star. The pole star was the symbolic axis of the wheeling firmament. It was of enormous importance in navigation, and many traditions revered it as the zenith of a supernatural pole or pillar linking the terrestrial and celestial spheres. The ancient Egyptians associated the pole star with the souls of their pharaohs; and the North Pole itself was linked with a spiritual centre in Masonic symbolism.

Moving stars symbolized the birth of gods in India as well as Western Asia. Here the Magi are guided to Jesus's birthplace by a star – thought by some to have been a comet.

PLANETS AS LIVING GODS

The ancient belief that planets were divinities has profoundly influenced the evolution of symbolism. For more than two thousand years after Greek writers incorporated this belief into their myths, leading thinkers in the fields of science, philosophy and religion continued to accept the principle that the planets presided over events on earth – as the sun and moon unarguably do. Although astrology and science had parted company by the 18th century, planetary symbolism had by then become an inextricable element of human life. The days of the week are themselves based on seven "planets" which the ancients could see moving busily against the vast backcloth of the stars. Taking the earth as the unmoving centre, these seven – a mystic number in consequence – included the Sun and Moon as well as Venus, Mercury, Mars, Jupiter and Saturn. To each were assigned characteristics based partly on their colour and motion, and partly on a system of "correspondences" to specific directions of space, colours, metals, bodily organs, jewels, flowers, and so on. All are distinctively personified in Western art.

The planet Venus presides over lovers in this 15th-century illustration. She appears as the evening star with some of her attributes including her signs, Libra and Taurus.

MERCURY usually appears as a youth with a caduceus, a winged cap and sandals, and is associated with mobility, mediation, reason, eloquence, free will, adaptation, commerce and the astrological signs Virgo and Gemini. **VENUS** is a beautiful woman associated with love (sacred or profane), desire, sexuality, pleasure, rebirth, imagination, harmony and happiness – although as Ishtar in Mesopotamia her morning aspect was linked with war. Her signs are Libra and Taurus. **MARS** is helmeted, armed with a shield and sword or spear and sometimes accompanied by a wolf. His associations are with energy, violence, courage, ardour, fire, and the signs Aries and Scorpio. **JUPITER** is an imposing, godlike man, often bearded. Attributes include the eagle, sceptre and thunderbolt. Associations include power, equilibrium, justice, optimism and the signs Sagittarius and Pisces. **SATURN** usually sports a grey beard and carries a sickle and often a crutch. Once associated with agriculture, he became more generally linked with pessimism, rigidity, morality, religion, chastity, contemplation, inertia, death and melancholy. His signs are Capricorn and Aquarius.

Sun

The sun is the dominant symbol of creative energy in most traditions, often worshipped as the supreme god or a manifestation of its all-seeing power. Some of the earliest graphic signs for the sun show it as the symbolic centre or heart of the cosmos. As the source of heat, it represents vitality, passion, courage and eternally renewed youth. As the source of light out of darkness, it symbolizes knowledge, intellect and truth personified. And as the most brilliant of the celestial bodies it is the emblem of royalty and imperial splendour.

The sun represents the male principle in most traditions, but was female in Germany and Japan and for many tribes in the Celtic world, Africa, Native America, Oceania and New Zealand. It was an imperial yang emblem in China but was never seen as supreme in the Chinese pantheon of gods. Like a number of other peoples, the Chinese symbolized the destructive aspects of solar power in a myth about how multiple suns made the world too hot. The ten original suns refused to share their solar duties on a rota basis and entered the sky together. The divine archer Yi had then to kill nine of them to restore cosmic balance. A distinctive solar emblem in China is a red disk with a three-legged black raven or crow symbolizing the three phases of the sun (rising, zenith, setting).

The most elaborate sun cults were those of Peru, Mexico and Egypt. Emphasizing the Inca claim to be "children of the sun", the Peruvian sun deity was depicted in human form with a disk-like golden face. In the Aztec cult of the Fifth Sun, the war god Huitzilopochtli required continuing human sacrifices to sustain the strength of

---

THE POWER OF THE DISK

This winged disk, which dates back to the 9th century BC, is the emblem of the great Assyrian god Asshur. The sun gods Ra and Ahura Mazda were also often represented by the winged disk.

The **DISK** is one of the oldest emblems of solar divinity and power. By adding wings to the disk, the ancients combined sun and eagle symbolism in an image of cosmic energy. This form of disk also incorporates the resurrection symbolism of the rising sun. In Egypt, the disk with horns or a crescent is a symbol of solar and lunar unity. A rayed disk in India is the weapon of Vishnu Surya, signifying his absolute power to destroy and create. Because the earliest wheels were solid, the disk can also represent the turning wheel of existence in Indian iconography, and often appears with the same wheel symbolism in illustrations showing the energy points of the chakras within the human body. In China, a disk with a central hole is a celestial image of spiritual perfection – the cosmic circle with the unknowable essence or void at its centre. Serpents or dragons encircling a disk represent the reconciliation of opposing forces.

the sun as guardian of the contemporary era. This charmless story, masking Aztec blood lust, is a pole away from the Nordic legend of the death of the handsome young Nordic god of light, Balder, but is one of countless myths and rites based on the symbolic theme of the sun's eclipse, nightly disappearances or seasonally waxing and waning power. Thus Egyptian solar mythology depicts the barque of the sun travelling each night through underworld perils before emerging triumphantly from the mouth of a serpent each morning. In a farcical treatment of the theme, the Japanese sun-goddess Amaterasu hides herself in a cave and has to be tricked to come out again. Personifications of the sun are multiple in some cultures, as in Egypt where Khepri is the scarab god of the rising sun, Horus the eye of day, Ra the zenith and Osiris the setting sun.

Alternatively, the sun is the son of the supreme god or symbolizes his vision or love. It was the eye of Zeus in Greece, of Odin in Scandinavia, of Ahura Mazda (or Ormuzd) in Iran, of Varuna in India and of Allah to Muhammad. It was the light of the Buddha, of the Great Spirit in Native North America, of God the Father in Christianity. Christ replaced Mithras in the Roman Empire as a resurrection symbol of the Unconquered Sun.

The solar cult of Mithras, Persian god of light, led the Romans to fix December 25 as his birthday. Christianity soon borrowed the date for its own god of light, Jesus Christ.

This Egyptian funerary stele from around 1,000BC depicts a woman before the falcon-headed god Ra-Horakhte – the manifestation of the rising sun – who radiates beneficial rays toward her.

In iconography, the sun is represented by a vast range of emblems. These include the gold disk, the rayed or winged disk (most common in the Middle East), the half-disk with rays (*Nihon*, meaning "sun-source", the emblem of Japan), the circle with central point (a symbol of the conscious self in astrology), and a star, spiral, ring, wheel, swastika or other turning cross form. In Western art, the sun can also be represented by the colours bronze, gold, yellow or red, a diamond, ruby, topaz, a winged or feathered serpent, an eagle, falcon, phoenix, swan, lion, ram, cock or bull.

Moon

The appearances and disappearances of the moon and its changes of form presented to early societies an impressive cosmic image of the earthly cycles of animal and vegetable birth, growth, decline, death and rebirth. The extent and power of lunar worship and symbolism is partly explained by the moon's importance as a source of light for night hunting and as the earliest measure of time – its phases forming the basis of the first known calendars. Beyond its influence on the tides, the moon was believed to control human destiny as well as rainfall, snow, floods, and the rhythms of plant and animal life in general, and of women in particular through the lunar rhythms of the menstrual cycle.

The Egyptian lunar god Khensu wears a crescent cradling the solar disc, symbolizing the divine unity of sun and moon.

Although primarily a symbol of the female principle, the moon was sometimes personified by male gods, especially among nomadic or hunting cultures. The moon was male in Japan, Oceania and the Teutonic countries as well, and also among some African and Native American tribes. Female moon deities vary in character, ranging from protective Great Mother goddesses to fierce, silvery defenders of their virginity such as the Roman hunter goddess Diana. Chastity, mutability, fickleness or "cold" indifference are all qualities associated with the moon. The "dark of the moon" (its three-day absence) made the moon a symbol of the passage from life to death as well as from death to life.

The Sumerian-Semitic moon god Sin, whose sign was a boat-shaped crescent, was Lord of Months and destiny. On this 12th-century BC *Babylonian stele, he receives a king and his daughter.*

Although generally a benevolent symbol across cultures, the moon can sometimes appear as an evil eye, a witching presence, by association with death and with sinister aspects of the night. Both the Egyptian god Thoth and the Greek goddess Hecate combined lunar and occult symbolism.

The full moon shares the symbolism of the circle as an image of wholeness or perfection. It is a Buddhist symbol of beauty and serenity, and, in China, of the completed family. The harvest moon (a full moon near the September equinox) is, for agricultural reasons, a fertility symbol, widely associated with love and marriage. The Chinese moon festival, held at the September equinox with fruits, sweetcakes and lanterns, also has fertility symbolism. The idea that the full moon brings on forms of madness other than love is of Roman origin (hence "lunatic"). Born idiots may be called "mooncalves" for the same reason, but also because the moon, presiding over dreams, is linked with fantasy or bemusement.

THE CRESCENT MOON

As an ancient symbol of cosmic power in western Asia, the crescent represented the boat of the moon god navigating the vast reaches of space. The Latin etymology of "crescent" (increasing) indicates why the crescent image was later used as a symbol of Islamic expansion, incorporating as it did the idea of the constantly regenerating moon.

From the time of the Crusades, the crescent became a counter-emblem to the Christian Cross – and the Red Crescent is the Islamic equivalent of the Red Cross today. Present-day countries that fly national flags bearing a crescent and one or more stars include Turkey, Libya, Tunisia and Malaysia.

Use of the crescent as an emblem long predated the Islamic empire. In Byzantium, coins were stamped with the crescent and star in 341BC when, according to one legend, the moon goddess Hecate intervened to save the city from Macedonian forces (their attack revealed by the sudden appearance of a crescent moon). The image of the crescent moon as a cup holding the elixir of immortality appears in Hindu and Celtic as well as Muslim traditions. In Egypt, the crescent and disk symbolized divine unity. The crescent moon is a long-standing symbol of the Great Mother, the Queen of Heaven; Greek and Roman lunar goddesses were depicted with a crescent in their hair, denoting chastity, and the Virgin Mary sometimes appears with a crescent at her feet in Christian iconography.

As the emblem of Islam, the crescent signifies divine authority, increase, resurrection and, with a star, paradise. The crescent on this 19th-century mosque lamp finial takes a horned form, itself symbolizing increase.

Time and the Seasons

Early measurements of **TIME** were based inescapably on cosmic events – the periods between the daily appearance and disappearance of the sun, the monthly phases of the moon, and the annual recurrence of the seasons. Each carried an enormous weight of symbolism. The **WEEK**, for example, is an artificial division of time, probably based on the fourfold division of the lunar cycle and the mystical significance of the number seven. This symbolism, enshrined in the Judeo-Christian seven-day week, was strong enough eventually to overcome the previous Roman custom of an eight-day week based on the old interval between market days. A further influence was the astrological system of seven "planets", which gave their names to the Latin days of the week – the moon, Mars, Mercury, Jupiter, Venus, Saturn and the sun.

The hourglass, a common symbol of time, became in Christian art a warning of life's brevity and the need for virtues such as temperance, personified here in Lorenzetti's Allegory of Good Government *from the 14th century.*

The Semitic tradition of dedicating the seventh day of each week to god is based on lunar symbolism dating back to Babylonian worship of the moon god Sin. Important state functions were suspended on this day in Babylon, suggesting to scholars the symbolism of an unpropitious "day out of time". In Judaism, the **SABBATH** became a symbol of God's Creation and of his covenant with the Israelites, commemorated in a festive day of rest on Saturday. Mainstream Christianity followed the established tradition of resting on the seventh day, but with less strict prohibitions, and on a Sunday – the emblematic day of Christ's resurrection. Islam also recognizes a seventh holy day of rest, but on a Friday.

In Japanese Buddhism, dawn, represented by the deity Amida, symbolizes ultimate enlightenment – an association suggested by the particular clarity of dawn light and its links with new beginnings.

The main phases of day each had their own symbolism. **DAWN** is an almost universal symbol of hope and youth. The Greek goddess of the dawn Eos (in Roman myth, Aurora) is usually shown as a winged goddess driving a chariot. Myth holds that she rode ahead of Helios, god of the sun, announcing his daily journey across the sky. Although dawn is linked with joy, Eos may also appear mourning her son Memnon, slain by the hero Achilles, her tears falling as dew.

NOON is the hour of revelation in Jewish and Islamic tradition and, more generally, the moment of naked confrontation. The positive spiritual significance of midday comes from the absence of shadows (which are considered harmful) and from ancient rituals of sun worship at the zenith when the sun appeared in its full power and glory. **TWILIGHT** is often linked with the half-light of decline and the shadowy border of death. In northern Europe, myths of the twilight of the gods – the German Götterdämmerung and the Nordic Ragnarök – symbolize the melancholy ebbing of solar warmth in a powerful image of the end of the world and the prelude to a fresh cycle of manifestation.

THE SEASONS IN WESTERN SYMBOLISM

Like the phases of the moon, the seasons were universal symbols of birth, growth, death and rebirth, the orderly cycles of nature and of human life. In Western art and astrology, **SPRING** is often shown as a child or young woman with sprigs of blossom. Associations are the Greek goddess Aphrodite, the Roman Flora, the lamb or kid, and the zodiac signs Aries, Taurus and Gemini. **SUMMER** is crowned with ears of corn and may carry a sickle. Links include the goddess Demeter (Ceres) or the god Apollo, the lion or dragon, and the signs Cancer, Leo and Virgo. **AUTUMN** usually has vine leaves, grapes and other fruit, perhaps in a cornucopia. Associations are Dionysus (Bacchus), the hare, and Libra, Scorpio and Sagittarius. **WINTER** may appear as an old man by a fire or a bare-headed woman in a winter landscape. Links are Hephaestus (Vulcan) or Boreas, the salamander or wild duck, and Capricorn, Aquarius and Pisces.

Flowers or crops handed from one figure to another in Walter Crane's The Seasons *convey the classical view of nature's cyclic continuity.*

Fire and Air

FIRE is a masculine and active element symbolizing both creative and destructive energy. Its wider symbolism includes purification, revelation, transformation, regeneration and spiritual or sexual ardour. Graphically, fire was represented by a triangle in alchemy, where it was the unifying element. On a domestic scale (the hearth fire), its image is protective and comforting; as a consuming force of nature it is threatening. For this reason, a duality of praise and fear underlay ritual fire worship.

In ancient or primitive cultures, fire appears to have been revered first as an actual god, later as a symbol of divine power. A seemingly living element, growing by what it fed on, dying and reappearing, it was sometimes interpreted as a terrestrial form of the sun, with which it shares much of its symbolism. Some fire cults were horrific – for example the Canaanite worship of "Moloch" to whom infants were sacrificed. The concept of purging evil by fire would later lead to the cruelest atrocities of the Christian Church. In Native North American traditions the campfire was an image of happiness and prosperity, and the sun itself was called the Great Fire. In Buddhism, a pillar of fire is one symbol of the Buddha, and fire as illumination can be a metaphor for wisdom. In mystical thought, fire often symbolizes union with the godhead, transcendence of the human condition, the end of all things. Hence the concept of the spiritual fire that burns without consuming – the "sages standing in God's holy fire" of W. B. Yeats's poem *Sailing to Byzantium*.

The resurrection symbolism of fire is personified by the phoenix and salamander. Regeneration symbolism also lies behind the Paschal rituals of both Roman Catholicism and Eastern Orthodox Churches in which candles are extinguished and then lit from "a new fire". New Year

Myths of heroes such as Prometheus stealing fire from the gods reflect the momentous importance of the discovery of fire-making. It seemed a god-like skill, and so fire symbolized divine energy.

Fire was personified in Central America by Huehueteotl, here shown as a toothless old man carrying a brazier on his head. He was one of the ancient gods, worshipped as man's earliest companion.

bonfires have their origin in forms of sympathetic magic, linking the making of new fires with the returning light and warmth of the sun. However, in Japan, Shinto fires at New Year are intended to forestall the risk of destructive fires in the year ahead.

The importance in primitive cultures of preserving domestic fires underlies the emblematic sacredness of an undying flame – as in the fire tended by the Vestal Virgins in Rome, or the modern Olympic tradition in which the flame carried to each new Games symbolizes the continuity of traditional sporting ideals. The purification symbolism of fire is still an important symbolic element in the practice of cremation. **SMOKE** itself is an ascension symbol – of purified souls or of prayers. In Native North America, smoke was a means of communication on a cosmic as well as a mundane level. Less often, it appears as a symbol of concealment or of the transitory nature of life.

In most cosmogonies, the primal element is **AIR** – equated with the soul by Stoic philosophers (followers of the Greek Zeno, in the 2nd century BC). Air shares much of the symbolism of breath and wind (which are easier for artists to depict). It is associated with freedom, purity and spiritual life.

SPIRITS OF THE WIND

Wind is a poetic image of the animating spirit whose effects can be seen and heard but who remains invisible. Wind, air and breath are closely allied in mystic symbolism, and the idea of the wind as cosmic animator, organizer or support was widespread. In the Bible, God speaks to Job from a whirlwind, and Genesis begins with His spirit moving like wind on the face of the deep. The Indo-Iranian wind god Vayu is cosmic breath. Below the elevated level of this symbolism, individual winds were often personified as violent and unpredictable. In Greek myth, to ensure the hero Odysseus had a calm voyage, Aeolus, master of the winds, gave them to him in a bag – which one of his crewmen disastrously opened. Demons were thought to ride violent winds, bringing evil and illness. In China, wind was associated with rumour, a symbolism derived from hunting and "getting wind of" a scent. Its importance in pollination also made it a sexual symbol. Wind is generally a powerful symbol of change, its dominant meaning in the 20th century.

Winds appear in many early cultures as symbolic messengers of divine forces that controlled the physical world. This was the origin of the puff-cheeked heads popular with early map-makers.

Thunder and Lightning

THUNDER was equated in Semitic and some other traditions with the voice of God. It is essentially a creative-destructive symbol, associated with an impregnating force as well as with chastisement or justice. Thus in Hindu and Buddhist tradition, Indra uses the *vajra*, a thunderbolt in the form of a diamond sceptre, to split the clouds, which represent ignorance in Tantric symbolism. The Inca rain god Ilyap'a releases the celestial waters with his thunder sling.

Although predominantly linked with male gods or with divine smiths, thunder was sometimes associated with earth or moon goddesses through its fecundity symbolism. In Asia (especially China), it was linked with the dragon. Some thunder gods, especially in Japan, were earth as well as sky deities, speaking from the volcano as well as from the clouds.

Thor's axe-hammer symbolized both thunder and lightning in Scandinavian mythology. But beyond its destructive power it was a protective emblem on gravestones and a fertility symbol in wedding rites.

LIGHTNING could also symbolize divine wrath or fertilizing potency. It was variously seen as the weapon, arm or phallus of the supreme male sky god – or of his auxiliary. Alternatively, it was the blinding light of his eye – in India the flashing third eye of Shiva, the light of truth.

Lightning is a rare example of a phenomenon symbolically linked with both fire and water because it often preceded rain, and as both creator and destroyer it was viewed with a mixture of fear and reverence. Places struck by lightning became sacred ground, and people it touched bore the mark of God if they survived, or were thought to be translated instantly to heaven if they died. In Mexico, for example, Tlaloc used lightning to despatch souls to the Aztec heaven.

Jewish tradition associated lightning with revelation, and it was widely thought to be an augury – significant enough in ancient Rome to cause public assemblies to close for the day.

In iconography, lightning is often represented by the flashing axe, the forked trident, the sceptre, the hammer, the arrow and graphically by the zigzag.

This wooden Kwakiutl Indian headdress from the northwest coast of America represents the mythical Thunderbird and had protective symbolism. Lightning was the blink of its eye, thunder the mighty concussion of its wings.

The fertility symbolism of lightning is particularly overt among the Australian Aboriginals, where it represents a cosmic erect penis. Hence the phallic motif skilfully blended into the pattern of this bark painting from western Arnhem Land, depicting Wala-Undayna (lightning man). One Greek myth claimed that Dionysus's mother was impregnated by a lightning flash from Zeus.

Rain, Clouds, Mist and Storms

RAIN has always been a vital symbol of fecundity, often linked in primitive agricultural societies with divine semen, as in Greek mythology. The early belief that the gods determine whether to withhold rain, unleash it with punishing force, or sprinkle it sweetly like a blessing, has been remarkably tenacious in the human mind. Gentle rain (likened to mercy by Portia in Shakespeare's *The Merchant of Venice*) was widely seen as a sign of divine approval or, in China, yin-yang harmony in the celestial sphere. The supreme fertility god of the Aztecs, Tlaloc (or Chac in the Mayan pantheon), was a rain god whose motif was a bar with comb-like teeth representing falling rain. To him children were sacrificed on mountain tops, their blood and tears propitious signs of coming rainfall.

A similar link between blood and rain appears in Iranian mythology where the rain god Tishtrya, embodied as a white

THE AMBIVALENT SYMBOLISM OF THE RAINBOW

As a sublime bridge between the supernatural and natural worlds, the rainbow is usually optimistic symbolically as well as meteorologically. It was a Hebrew sign of God's reconcilement with terrestrial life after the Flood and of his covenant with the Jews. In Greece, the rainbow goddess Iris, robed in iridescent dew, carried messages to earth from the supreme god Zeus and his wife Hera. In India the rainbow was the bow of the hero-god Indra (a tradition paralleled in the Pacific where the rainbow is the emblem of Kahukara, the Maori war god). In Tibetan Tantric Buddhism the "rainbow body" is the penultimate transitional state of meditation in which matter begins to be transformed into pure light. Because it combines solar and water symbolism, the rainbow touching the earth suggested prosperity as well as fertility – the folklore "pot of gold". In some early cultures, an underworld symbolism appears. The rainbow was associated with a serpent in parts of Africa, India, Asia, North America and Australia, and its powers were unpredictable. In central African myths, Nkongolo, the Rainbow King, is a cruel tyrant. Hence, perhaps, the African and Asian superstition that it was provocative to point at a rainbow. In central Asia, rainbow-coloured ribbons were a shamanistic aid to sky travel, but there were folklore warnings against treading on the end of a rainbow and being whirled upward. In Buddhism, the ladder symbolism of the rainbow is positive.

A rainbow band encloses two divinities flanking the sacred maize plant, which is their gift to humanity, in this 19th-century Navaho blanket based on a sand painting design.

Gustav Klimt's painting shows Danae, mother of the Greek hero Perseus, being impregnated by Zeus in the form of a golden shower – an erotic image of rain's divine fertility symbolism.

horse, is sustained by sacrifices as he fights the black horse of drought. The heavenly origin of rain also made it an emblem of purity, and purification rituals were often carried out to invoke its fall. In the straightforward sympathetic magic of rain dancing, stamping feet imitated the patter of drops striking the earth. Apart from the axe, hammer and thunderbolt (a rain of fire or light), symbols of rain include the snake or horned serpent, the dragon in China, frogs and other amphibians, lunar creatures such as the crab and spider, dogs (associated with wind gods) and, more unexpectedly, the cat, chameleon, cow, elephant, parrot and turkey. Folklore associations of the spider with coming rain (and by extension with wealth) are particularly widespread, a symbolism that may be suggested by the spider descending its thread, emblematically bringing heavenly gifts.

CLOUDS themselves inevitably had fecundity symbolism. In ancient societies, their modern associations with gloom, obscurity or depression seldom appeared. Apart from their role as harbingers of rain, clouds also stood for revelation, a divinity almost made manifest. Thus Jehovah guided the Israelites as a pillar of cloud, and Allah speaks from a cloud in the Koran. Clouds, especially pink ones, are symbols of happiness in China, and also emblems of ascent to heaven. "Cloud Nine" is mystical bliss.

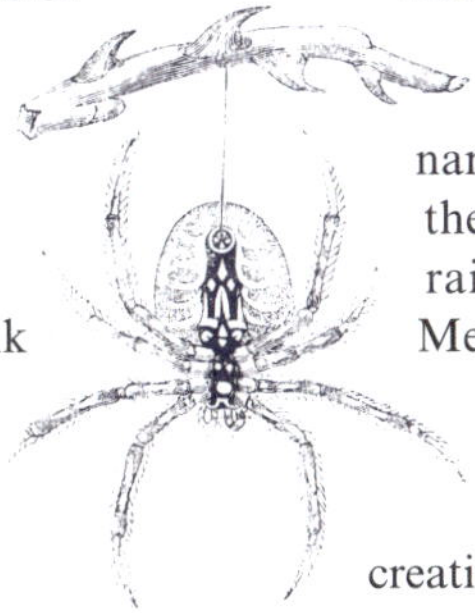

Supernatural intervention is associated with **MIST**, especially in Chinese landscape painting where it often has this symbolic meaning in scenes of paradisal gardens. In traditional symbolism generally, mist can stand for the indeterminate, a prelude to revelation or to the emergence of new forms, as in initiation rites.

The devastation sometimes wrought by a **STORM** made it a symbol of divine anger or punishment in most parts of the world. But storms, too, suggested creative energy and fecundity to ancient peoples. Hence the name "house of abundance" for the temple of Hadad, the great rain-bringing storm-god of Mesopotamia. Most storm gods that are depicted in myth wielding axes, hammers or thunderbolts have dual creative-destructive symbolism.

Water

Nearly all ancient cosmologies associate **WATER** with purity, fertility and the source of life. The **SEA** is a maternal image even more primary than the earth. It is a symbol of formless potentiality, an emblem of fluidity, dissolution, mingling, cohesion, birth and regeneration. The *Rig Veda* sings the praises of water as the bringer of all things.

The purest waters – especially **DEW** and **SPRING WATER** – were thought to have numinous and curative properties as forms of divine grace, gifts of Mother Earth (spring water) or sky gods (rain and dew). Reverence for fresh water as a purifying element is particularly marked in the religious traditions of countries where water was scarce, as Islamic, Jewish, Christian and Indian cleansing or baptism rituals show. Flood myths in which a sinful society is destroyed are examples of cleansing and regeneration symbolism. The transition symbolism of water accounts for numerous mythologies in which rivers or seas divide the worlds of the living and the dead.

Many divinities are water-born or walk on water. In superstition, the purity symbolism of water was so strong that it was thought to reject evil. Hence the custom of identifying witches by hurling women in ponds to see if they floated to the surface. Water is also equated with wisdom, as in the Taoist image of water finding its way around obstacles, the triumph of seeming weakness over strength. In psychology it represents the energy of the unconscious and its mysterious depths and perils. Restless water is a Buddhist symbol of the agitated flux of manifestation. By contrast, the transparency of still water symbolizes contemplative perception.

Rushing torrents like this mountain stream are powerful natural symbols of the flowing away of all things – the passage of time and life.

In legend and folklore, **LAKES** are two-way mirrors dividing natural and supernatural worlds, the reflective surface suggesting both contemplation from above and observation from below by spirits thought to inhabit jewelled palaces. The Celtic custom of casting trophies to these spirits explains the connection between the Lady of the Lake and the sword Excalibur in Arthurian legend. Mythical lake and spring divinities, traditionally youthful and with

Baptism combines the purifying, dissolving and fertilizing aspects of water symbolism – initiating a new life, as in this 14th-century French illumination, or effacing an old one by washing away sin.

The Roman god Neptune embodied the cosmic power fertilizing the sea. He was also the god of white horses – breaking waves – which he spurred on with his trident.

prophetic or healing powers, were often propitiated with gifts – the origin of throwing coins in fountains and making wishes. In myth, folklore and religion, **SPRINGS** are magical or spiritually significant places, an idea based partly on the general symbolism of water and partly on the spring as the unpolluted origin of water. The healing properties of mineral springs may have added to the curative symbolism of springs in general. A spring flowing from the Tree of Life fed the four rivers of paradise – a Christian symbol of salvation. In Norse myth, the god Odin gives one of his eyes for a draught of water from the Fountain of Knowledge flowing from the world axis, the tree Yggdrasil. Water rising from the earth symbolized feminine bounty.

SACRED RIVERS

For the many great civilizations dependent on their irrigating fertility, rivers were important symbols of supply as well as purification and removal. The common image of four streams in paradise flowing from the Tree of Life to the cardinal points was a metaphor for divine energy and spiritual nourishment coursing through the whole universe.

In Hinduism, the Ganges, personified by the supreme river goddess Ganga, was an axial symbol, depicted in myth as falling from heaven to cleanse the earth and penetrating also to the underworld. Purification in the Ganges is a central ritual in Hinduism. A cruder example of purification symbolism appears in the Greek myth of Herakles who diverted a river through the Augean stables. Because they were unpredictable, rivers were propitiated with sacrifices to local gods or, more usually, goddesses. They often appear as boundaries, particularly dividing the worlds of the living and the dead. The Celts thought river confluences were particularly sacred. In China, the drowned were thought to haunt rivers, hoping to find living bodies they could inhabit.

Akbar, greatest of the Mughal Emperors, would have been well aware of the central symbolism of the Ganges in Hindu religion when he began his conquest of Northern India in the 1550s. This illustration from the Akbarnama *(his memoirs) shows him ceremonially fording the river with a herd of elephants.*

Earth, Caves and Stone

The **EARTH** is a symbol of fecundity, sustenance and protection, usually personified in mythology by mother goddesses, such as the classical Ge or Gaia. In many creation myths, the first humans are formed from mud, clay or, in Polynesia, sand. The sky couples with the earth – sometimes in an embrace so close that it must be broken by a hero-god to allow life to develop – an idea common to Polynesian and Egyptian myth. Fecundity and regeneration symbolism account for the use of earth in rites of passage, where initiates are "buried" and dug up again. Couplings in furrows were a feature of rural life at spring fertility festivities until fairly recently.

As a fixed principle, the earth is often symbolized graphically by a square. Although associated with passivity and darkness it is usually separated in symbolism from the underworld as a source of life rather than an abode of the dead. The Aztec goddess of the earth and childbirth, Cihuacoatl, fed on the dead to nourish the living, but more usually earth symbolism is gentle. Hence, perhaps, the widespread ancient notion that destructive earthquakes emanated not from the earth but from the movements of creatures thought to support it – a giant fish (Japan), an elephant standing on a tortoise (India) or a serpent (North America).

Of all earth's features, the most primal symbol of shelter is the **CAVE**, a womb image of birth, rebirth, the origin and the centre. Caves can also have darker meanings: the underworld, the entrance to hell and, in psychology, regressive wishes or the unconscious itself.

A mountain cave is the setting for Watteau's image of the first Christian monk's battle for self-control, The Temptation of St Antony.

More usually, as widely expressed in myths and initiation rites, caves were places where the germinating powers of the earth were concentrated, where oracles spoke, where initiates were reborn in spiritual understanding, and where souls ascended to celestial light. Sacred caves and grottoes, usually on hills or mountains were ritually used as earth-to-sky axial symbols and were the focus of spiritual forces, often represented by a pillar or lingam.

In folklore, caves can symbolize less ethical goals – the treasures of Aladdin, for example – protected by dragons or cunning gnomes. In Turkic myth, a cave is the birthplace of the first man.

Maternal goddesses such as the Vedic Maja, here shown within a globe, frequently personify the earth, which is seen symbolically as the protective womb of life.

THE MAGICAL POWER OF THE STONE

Stone is a compelling animist symbol of forces thought to exist within inanimate matter. In ancient cultures, the general qualities of rock – permanence, strength, integrity – were heightened and given sacred significance in individual standing stones, sacrificial stone axes or knives, and stone objects such as amulets. Stones stored heat, coldness, water and (as jewels) light. In Native North America, they were the metaphoric bones of Mother Earth, as also in Greece and in Asia Minor where the great mother goddess Cybele was worshipped in the form of a stone. As durable symbols of life force, stones were used to mark sacred places. Stones, such as the altar, omphalos or lingam, served as a focus for sacrifice or worship. Sacrificial victims were bound to them or (in Fiji) had their brains dashed out on them. In funerary memorials, stone still symbolizes eternal life. In coronation rituals, stone objects could signify authority hallowed by tradition. For example, to symbolize his claim to suzerainty over Scotland, Edward I stole the Stone of Scone on which Scots kings had been crowned until 1296 and installed it at Westminster. The tradition of kissing a stone at Blarney Castle to acquire "the gift of the gab" is based on the oracular symbolism of stone not only in Celtic tradition but also elsewhere.

The colossal statues of Easter Island are among the most remarkable of many giant standing stones that appear as lifelike presences testifying to the steadfastness of the human spirit.

Mountains

As the meeting-place of earth and heaven, the mountain is a symbol of transcendence, eternity, purity and spiritual ascent. The belief that deities inhabited mountains or manifested their presence there was once universal in countries with peaks high enough to be veiled by clouds. Such mountains were often feared as well as venerated – as in Africa. They were associated with immortals, heroes, sanctified prophets and gods. The Bible is full of references to sacred mountains. God's revelations to Moses and Elijah on Mt Sinai were paralleled in Christianity by Christ's transfiguration, when he went with a few disciples "up a mountain to pray". It was on Mt Carmel that Elijah triumphed over the priests of Baal, and on the Mount of Olives that Christ ascended into heaven according to the Acts of the Apostles. In medieval legends of the Grail, the elixir of life is guarded in a castle on Montsalvat. In China, the World Mountain, Kunlun, thought to be the source of the Yellow River, was a symbol of order and harmony, the dwelling-place of immortals and of the Supreme Being. In Central Mexico, Mt Tlaloc was a personification of the great fertility and rain god. From Mt Olympus, the Greeks were subject to the whims of their quarrelsome gods. Sacred mountains could be figurative as well as real, as in the Celtic White Mountain, the emerald-based Qaf of Islam, or Mt Meru, the Hindu World Mountain at the North Pole. In Hindu cosmogony, Mt Mandara is used as a pivot to churn the cosmic waters. The polar mountain was seen as a world axis. The peak of a great mountain could symbolize a point of departure from terrestrial life. Sometimes the mountain was hollow, and contained sleeping immortals. Figurative mountains were usually envisaged as layered, representing progressive stages of spiritual ascent. Mountain-shaped temples express the same idea in the great ziggurats of Mesopotamia or Central America and in the stupas and pagodas of Asia. Verticality makes the mountain a masculine symbol, although the great mother goddess Cybele was specifically a mountain deity. In art, twin-peaked mountains are sometimes used to symbolize dual powers. Other mountain symbols include the triangle, cross, crown, star and steps or ladders. Muhammad reputedly used the immutability of mountains as an allegory of the need for humility when he ordered Mt Safa to move: when it refused to budge he went to the mountain to thank God that it had stayed put.

Fujiyama, or Mount Fuji is almost an emblem of Japan itself. It was and remains a sacred place of Shinto pilgrimage. Psychologically, climbing the mountain (no mean feat because Fuji's height is 12,400ft, or 3,776m) symbolizes a supreme challenge, the stages toward spiritual self-knowledge.

Edward Lear's painting depicts Mount Sinai where, according to the Old Testament, Moses received from God two tablets of stone on which were inscribed the Ten Commandments.

Metals and Precious Stones

The ancients believed **METALS** were a solid form of cosmic energy – a symbolism that explains some puzzling aspects of ancient attitudes toward them. Metals, like humans, were earthly things with celestial potential. Hence the development of a cosmic hierarchy in which metals were paired with the seven known planets.

GOLD was a metal of perfection, symbolically divine through its universal association with the sun in the ancient world and also because of its remarkable lustre, resistance to rust, durability and malleability. Its associated emblematic qualities range from purity, refinement, spiritual enlightenment, truth, harmony and wisdom to earthly power and glory, majesty, nobility and wealth. Gold was the preferred metal for sacred objects or for sanctified kings. In the Inca empire, acceding rulers were covered in resin sprayed with gold dust, the historical origin of El Dorado (the gilded man). Gilding on the icons of Byzantine Christianity and of Buddhism symbolized divinity, as does the gold-leaf work of medieval art. Gold was the faeces of the sun god Huitzilopochtli in Aztec Mexico – or was thought to be a residue of the sun itself, its illumination left as threads in the earth, a mineral form of

JADE, THE LAPIDARY STONE OF CHINA

Chinese tradition associated jade with a whole spectrum of virtues: moral purity, justice, truth, courage, harmony, loyalty and benevolence. The imperial jade seal symbolized a celestial mandate. The many hues of jade, ranging from white through green, blue and red to near-black, allowed religious objects to be distinguished by colour as well as shape. The Ts'ung emblem of the earth was a yellow cone within a rectangular body.

A famous Chinese religious jade object is the Pi emblem of the Gate of Heaven – a blue-green perforated disk, as in this 4th century BC example.

Although a solar and yang emblem, the lustrous smoothness of jade linked it also with the soft beauty of female flesh, mucus (jade juice) and sexual intercourse itself (jade play). The hardness and durability of nephrite (the material of most Chinese jade carving until the 18th century) led by sympathetic magic to the belief that jade amulets could preserve the body after death – hence the number of jade objects found in tombs. Chinese alchemists believed jade to be a perfected form of stone, replacing gold as an emblem of ultimate purity.

Jade in the form of green nephrite had similarly high value in ancient Mexico, where it was a symbol of the heart and of blood through its association with fertilizing waters. Among the New Zealand Maori, the beautiful green nephrite pounamu, found in the South Island, was used to make the sacred *mere*, a war club symbolizing authority.

In many traditions, gold was identified as the actual substance of divinity – the flesh of Ra in Egypt. In this wall painting from a tomb (c.1400BC), Nubian tribute-bearers bring gifts of gold for the pharaoh.

light, as in Hindu thought. Alternatively, it was a symbol of the spirit of enlightenment, as in Buddhism, or of Christ's message. By association with the sun, gold became a strong masculine symbol. Most of the metal's symbolism also attaches to the colour gold.

SILVER could also symbolize purity, as well as chastity and eloquence. Seen as a lunar, feminine and cold metal, it was the attribute of moon goddesses (in particular the Roman Diana) and of queens. Through its link with the moon it was equated also with the light of hope and with wisdom – orators are silver-tongued.

MERCURY (the metal, planet and god) has consistent and universal symbolism in mythology, astrology and alchemy. It symbolizes fluidity, liaison, transformation and the intellect; it is also known as quick ("active") silver. The planet Mercury circles the sun quickly and is elusive to observe, hence its association with the mythical winged messenger of the gods (Hermes/Mercury).

Meteoric **IRON** was prized as a celestial metal, especially by the Aztecs, but smelted iron was seen as an instrument of evil. This symbolism suggests that the ancients thought iron vulgar compared to **COPPER** and **BRONZE**, let alone gold, all of which were preferred for religious artefacts.

Stones associated with religion or ritual include **LAPIS LAZULI**, a blue stone with celestial symbolism; **TURQUOISE**, a solar and fire symbol in Mexico; and **CRYSTAL**, linked with spiritual perfection. Crystal symbolized the notion of looking beyond the material world and was an emblem of shamanistic powers. Hence the appearance of magical crystal slippers in folklore.

Early smelting techniques and efforts to refine base metals made metallurgy an allegory of spiritual purification. Gold became the alchemical Great Work, the goal of the transformation process.

Minerals of luminous brilliance, embedded in the earth, were a source of wonder to early societies worldwide – evidence of divine energy, working in the darkness of the earth to produce perfected stones of light. Accordingly, **JEWELS** became symbols of spiritual illumination, purity, refinement, superiority or durability and were ascribed magical powers of healing and protection. In Eastern religion they embody the treasures of spiritual knowledge, or divine union (the jewel in the lotus). Specific gemstones inevitably have their own associations – for example, reflective or transparent stones are linked with divination, and red ones with ardour or vitality.

The fertility symbolism of the **EMERALD** was probably based on its vernal green colour. It was an important stone in Aztec mythology, associated with the green-plumaged quetzal, harbinger of spring, and thus with the hero-god Quetzalcoatl. There and elsewhere it was associated with the moon, rain, water and the east. It is a Christian symbol of immortality, faith and hope, and the stone of the pope. Its extensive role in folklore as a healing amulet mingles fertility symbolism with a tradition of occult power which could be used for good or evil purposes, deriving from the story that it is an underworld stone, fallen from the crown of Lucifer.

The **DIAMOND** symbolizes radiance, immutability and integrity. Its combination of brilliance and hardness gave it a spiritual dimension, particularly in India where the diamond throne of the Buddha is an image of the unchanging Buddhist centre, and the diamond sceptre a Tantric symbol of divine power. In Western tradition the diamond symbolizes incorruptibility and thus virtues such as sincerity and constancy – hence its use in engagement rings.

The **RUBY** stands for love, vitality, royalty and courage. It is the stone of fortune and happiness (including longevity) in India, Burma, China and Japan. Its colour, ranging from red to the purplish "pigeon's blood" hue of the most valuable rubies,

Twelve jewels symbolized truth on the breastplate of the Jewish High Priest. But sexual enticement is the more likely reason for the gems bedecking Salome as she dances here for Herod.

THE CELESTIAL PEARL

Symbolically combining fire and water, the pearl is an Oriental yin-yang emblem, as in this mother-of-pearl inlay. It may symbolize lightning when shown with dragons (thunder).

The pearl is the quintessential symbol both of light and of femininity – its pale iridescence associated with the luminous moon, its watery origins with fertility, its secret life in the shell with miraculous birth or rebirth.

Hidden light also made the pearl a symbol of spiritual wisdom or esoteric knowledge. As a form of celestial light, the pearl is the third eye (spiritual illumination) of Shiva and of the Buddha. Transfiguration symbolism led to the expensive Asian funerary custom of placing a pearl in the mouth of the dead. In the afterlife, pearls formed the individual spheres enclosing the Islamic blessed – and the gates of the new Jerusalem (in Revelation).

Pearls were thought to be medicinal as well as sacred. The Romans, who wore pearls in homage to Isis, used them as talismans against everything from shark attacks to lunacy, and powdered pearl is still an Indian panacea. In classical tradition, pearls were worn by the love goddess Aphrodite (in Roman myth, Venus). Yet they can also symbolize purity and innocence. Their association with tears made them an unlucky bridal jewel – a broken pearl necklace was particularly ominous. In the ancient world, pearls were also, of course, straightforward symbols of wealth. Cleopatra reputedly dropped a pearl earring in her wine and drank it to show Antony how rich she was.

---

linked it in the classical world with the fiery Ares (in Roman myth, Mars), but also with Cronos (Saturn), who controlled passion. It was said to inflame lovers and was believed to glow in the dark. Homeopathically, the ruby was a medicinal jewel, thought to be effective for loss of blood as well as low spirits. Fire is the symbolism of its appearance on the foreheads of legendary dragons.

AMETHYST symbolizes temperance, peace, humility and piety – a stone attuned to the Age of Aquarius. Bishops wore it because of its modest violet or cool purple colour, and the Greek belief that it promoted sobriety – *amethustos* meaning "not intoxicated". As talismans, these stones were thought to promote wholesome dreams. In stone lore, the **SAPPHIRE** is an emblem of celestial harmony, peace, truth and serenity. A jewel of heaven, the sapphire was sacred to the planet Saturn in Hindu tradition and was therefore associated with self-control.

This heart brooch exploits the ruby's symbolism as a stone of lovers. Catherine of Aragon's ruby reputedly faded as she lost favour with Henry VIII.

Arts and Artefacts

Craftsmen not only create representational images of symbols taken from the natural world but also give symbolic form to many utilitarian artefacts. These range from the architecture of the great temples and public buildings to the most humble implements, weapons, clothes or accessories used in daily life. Symbolism attaches itself quickly to some man-made things. For example, flags, originally designed for identification, rapidly became sacred symbols of supremacy. A less obvious example is the conversion of a tobacco pipe into a calumet – the ceremonial pipe of Native North America, symbolizing the union of nature and spirit, man and god. Its smoking could signify peace (a white-feathered stem), but also war (red); more generally it was a sign of hospitality. The smoke, symbolizing vital breath, was ceremonially puffed toward the sky, the earth and the four cardinal points.

The calumet not just a pipe, it was a medium of prayer, just as the jaguar throne shown below was not so much a seat as an emblem of a Mayan ruler's power.

Prayer flags leading to Leh monastery in Ladakh draw on the ancient use of banners as a means of communicating with gods or spirits of the elements. The unseen air currents that move the flags symbolize a world beyond the visible.

Monuments and Buildings

Throughout history, the functional forms of sacred buildings have been profoundly modified by their symbolic purpose – to represent divine power and order. This is as true of simple temples as it is of the tiered ziggurats, stupas and pagodas of Eastern tradition or the glories of Western temples in the classical, Romanesque, Gothic, Renaissance and baroque periods.

In Egypt, the **PYRAMID** was a "hill of light" – symbol of the creative power of the sun and the immortality of his earthly representative, the pharaoh it entombed. It was developed from the conventional flat-topped mastaba tomb by Imhotep, the high priest of the sun god Ra. Although his pyramid for the pharaoh Zoser at Saqqara was stepped, later architects perfected the form of the true pyramid, facing it with limestone to reflect the light, clarifying its symbolism. It represented the primal mound which, in Egyptian cosmogony,

STUPAS AND PAGODAS

The **STUPA** is a domed reliquary built as a symbol of the Buddha's teaching – the renunciation of earthly desires. In its classic form based on the simple tumulus grave, a square base symbolizes the terrestial plane, a dome the cosmic egg, surmounted by a balcony representing the 33 heavens ruled by Shiva. The whole is penetrated by an axial mast with rings or parasols symbolizing the Buddha's ascent and escape from the round of existence.

An alternative form of sacred building in the Buddhist tradition is the **PAGODA**, a more vertical symbol of the Buddha and of heavenly ascent through progressive stages of enlightenment. The tiered pagoda, widely found in southeast Asia, China and Japan, was based on an Indian temple near Peshawar. It was the prototype for the conical stupa or sacred funeral mound, which is an architectural diagram of the cosmos. The tiers rising in diminishing scale represent the steps up the World Mountain or the axis linking earth and sky. The word *pagoda* is thought to be a Portugese corruption of the Sanskrit word *bhagavati* ("of the divine").

The Thieu Mu Pagoda in Vietnam shows the simplest form of Asian temple-mountain, spiritual ascent symbolized by diminishing tiers.

In Hebrew tradition, the chief ziggurat of Babylon was the Tower of Babel, an emblem of human pride and folly carrying the axial earth–heaven symbolism of the tower to insolent heights.

first caught the light of the creator sun. The mass and power of the structure were "material for eternity" – a building whose permanence negated death.

The **ZIGGURAT**, a massive Mesopotamian stepped temple built of brick symbolized a sacred mountain. Spiritually, the ziggurats, built between about 2200 and 500BC, represented both human ascension (via the staircases to rising levels) and the hope that the gods to whom they were individually dedicated would descend to the sanctuaries at the top. Ziggurats were typically built on seven levels, representing the seven heavens and planes of existence. Ziggurat-like stepped temples in Mesoamerica also had planetary significance.

Emblematically, the **TABERNACLE** of Hebrew tradition was the earthly throne or dwelling-place of God – a sanctuary, originally established by Moses in the wilderness according to precise geometric rules. Symbolizing the cosmos, it was centred upon a Holy of Holies containing the Ark of the Covenant and approached through a series of veiled spaces of increasing sanctity.

The **PILLAR** symbolizes stability – the idea of standing firm in the face of adversity and change. In the ancient world, pillars often had emblematic significance, representing divine power and authority or vital energy. In Egypt the *djed* pole (a pillar eventually embellished with four capitals) was said to represent the spinal column of the god Osiris, which channeled energy between sky and earth. Mesopotamian and Phoenician gods were similarly represented by pillars, sometimes topped by emblems such as the ram's head of the great Ea. At Carthage, three pillars symbolized the moon and its phases. The role of the pillar as a symbol of communication with supernatural forces is also clear in pre-Columbian cultures, as at Machu Picchu in Peru, where Inca priests ritually "tied" their sun god to a pillar.

The **OBELISK** was an Egyptian symbol of the sun god Ra in the form of a rectangular, tapering pillar topped by a reflective pyramid designed to catch and concentrate the light. A broken pillar or pole was a symbol of death or chaos not only in Western art but also for the Aborigines of Australia.

The bright castle of legend symbolizes the goal of a spiritual quest or, in art, may stand for Chastity – well defended.

Lamps, Utensils and Tools

The positive cosmic symbolism of light attached itself to many man-made objects. As an image of spiritual illumination in the darkness of ignorance, the **CANDLE** is an important emblem in Christian ritual, standing for Christ, the Church, joy, faith and witness. At a more personal level, the short-lived candle and its easily extinguished flame became a metaphor for the solitary, aspiring human soul. The **LAMP** or **LANTERN** symbolizes spirit, truth and life itself. The Arabian Nights tale of Aladdin who allowed his magic lamp to rust after it had brought him riches is an allegory of neglecting the spiritual side of life. In shrines or on altars, lamps symbolize both devotion and the presence of divinity. In art, they personify vigilance.

The mirror is one of the Eight Precious Things of Chinese Buddhism. It is also an emblem of sincerity and marital harmony, and a charm against evil.

An everyday household object with an vast range of symbolism is the **MIRROR** – an emblem of veracity, self-knowledge, purity, enlightenment and divination. Again, its positive meanings depend on its ancient association with light, especially the light of the mirror-like disks of the sun and moon, thought to reflect divinity to earth. Hence the belief that evil spirits could not abide mirrors and, as spirits of darkness, had no reflection. Although mirrors sometimes appear in Western art as disapproving attributes of pride, vanity or lust, they more often symbolize truth – the folk wisdom that the mirror never lies. The philosophical significance of the mirror as a symbol of the self-examined life is widespread in Asian traditions and particularly important in Japanese myth and religion.

Almost everywhere, mirrors have been linked with magic and especially with divination because they can reflect past or future events as well as present ones. The widespread superstition that breaking a mirror brings seven years of bad luck is linked with primitive ideas that a person's

The Menorah is the seven-branched candlestick of the Jewish religion. Its seven branches represent the planets, the days of the week and the seven levels of heaven

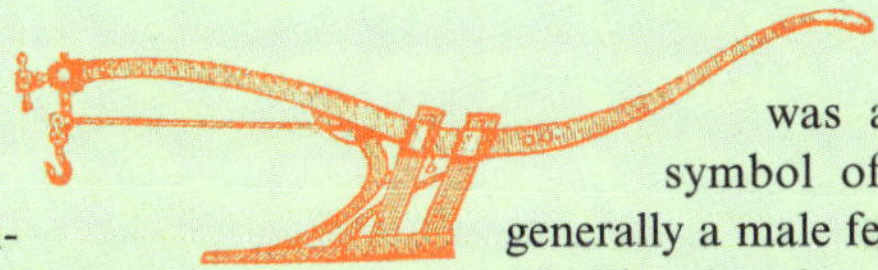

reflection contains part of his or her life force, or a twin "soul".

Containers with feminine symbolism such as **CUPS**, **URNS** or **VASES** often appear as emblems of eternal life in art or in funerary practices. A goblet with specific symbolism is the **CHALICE**, associated with the legend of the Holy Grail. It symbolizes the drinking in of spiritual illumination or knowledge, redemption, and hence immortality. The chalice appears in art as an emblem of faith and is an attribute of several saints.

The **PLOUGH** was an Old Testament symbol of peace and more generally a male fertility symbol – the phallic plough entering the female earth. Ritual ploughing by a new Chinese emperor symbolized his responsibility for the fertility of his country. Nomadic peoples once saw ploughing as an affront to the integrity of Mother Earth. The **YOKE** became a symbol of oppression after the Romans humiliated defeated armies by making them pass under a yoke-shaped structure denoting enslavement.

THE MAGIC CAULDRON

The cauldron's ancient links with magic probably originated with its capacity to produce surprising quantities of food and to turn everyday nourishing materials into gastronomic marvels. It was only a step from this to the belief that it could brew up magic potions or hell-broths. As a result it gathered a wide range of emblematic meanings including transformation, germination, plenty, and the possibility of rebirth or rejuvenation. False hope of their father's rejuvenation led the daughters of King Pelias of Iolcus in Thessaly to chop him up and throw the pieces into a cauldron on the treacherous advice of the sorceress Medea. Also in Greek myth, Thetis, the mother of Achilles, lost several earlier children when she put them in a cauldron to find out if they had inherited her immortality or were mortal like their father. A Kirghiz epic features a magic blood-drinking cauldron which the hero must recover from the bottom of the ocean. Underwater cauldrons appear in Celtic myth. The most prized possession of the Irish father god Dagda was a life-giving cauldron (Undry) that could never be emptied. The midnight hags of Shakespeare's *Macbeth* (*c.*1606–7) threw "eye of newt and toe of frog" into their witch-brew, thus following a long tradition of belief in the magical properties of the cauldron. More cruelly, the cauldron could also be used as an instrument of torture, making it a symbol of initiation, trial or punishment.

Christian legend includes a number of tales of saints boiling in cauldrons. St John the Evangelist is said to have survived such a spiritual trial.

Weapons

In the ancient world, where life was uncertain, **WEAPONS** were necessary defences, and some, like the hammer and axe, were used to create as well as destroy. As a result, their symbolism is seldom wholly aggressive. Many are linked with truth, aspiration or other virtues, and in myths and legends magical ones are given to heroes. Weapons often became ceremonial emblems of authority or justice. The **MACE** in the British House of Commons is such an example. Weapons are shown being broken or burned in allegories of peace

The **HAMMER** was a symbol of male strength, linked with the power of the sun and with gods of war, but also with beneficent artisan gods in its role as a tool rather than a weapon. Even the mighty stone hammer of the Nordic god Thor appeared as a protective emblem on gravestones and as a symbol of authority on marriage contracts. In the hands of the Greek god Hephaestus (Vulcan), the hammer was an instrument of divine skill, an emblem of the creative vigour that drives the chisel or shapes metal. This is the meaning of its use in Freemasonry as an attribute of the Lodge Master, symbolizing creative intelligence. In China the hammer was a symbol of the sovereign power to shape society. There and in India, its destructiveness was linked with the conquest of evil. The **CLUB** had a similar dual role and in art can represent either brutality or heroism. The **AXE** is a near-universal symbol of decisive power, linked with ancient sun and storm gods and with chiefly authority. Its flashing, thudding, spark-striking fall explains much of its symbolic associations with fire and also with the creative, germinating force of the thunderbolt; it was used directly to invoke thunder and rain in West Africa. Axes were used to split the skulls of sacrificial oxen in the Middle East, and are an attribute of several martyred Christian saints, notably Matthew. The axe also represents the forceful solving of a problem: it severs the round of Buddhist existence; symbolizes the union of families in Chinese

The lance, here wielded by a 15th-century Italian prince, is linked with the symbolism of the knight as a master of horsemanship and weaponry, a spiritually tested man of honour.

A noisy tool, the hammer was associated by the Celts with thunder and by extension with fecundity – the release of rain or the cracking of ice in spring.

marriages; and cures the headache of Zeus in the Greek legend in which Athene springs from a cleft in his head. The double-headed axe sometimes carved into Minoan building blocks may invoke the protection of Zeus. Alternatively, its dual, half-moon curves may be a lunar symbol or may stand for the reconciliation of opposites.

Subramanja, Vedic god of victory, is one of several war gods shown in Indian iconography riding a peacock. He has multiple arms and weapons to symbolize invincible power.

The **LANCE** was the stock weapon of the cavalry until the 20th century. It is associated with chivalry and with Christ's Passion because a centurion pierced His side with a lance on the cross. Like the **SPEAR**, it is more commonly a symbol of masculine, phallic and earthly power. The broken lance is an attribute of St George, and symbolizes the experienced soldier.

The **TRIDENT** became a specific symbol of sea power, most famously carried by the Roman god Neptune. It was an emblem of the ancient Minoan civilization, and more recently of Britannia ruling the waves.

BOW AND ARROW

The **BOW** symbolizes stored energy, willpower, aspiration, divine or terrestial power, and dynamic tension, especially sexual. As humanity's most effective long-range weapon for many millennia, the bow is an obvious emblem of war and hunting, but the control needed to master it gave it a deeper significance. In Oriental thought, particularly, it represented spiritual discipline, the combination of force and composure extolled as a samurai virtue. A Homeric test of fitness to rule (as exemplified by the bow that only Odysseus could draw), the bow is also an attribute of the Greek god of light, Apollo, a symbol of the sun's fertilizing power. Paintings of gods of love with bows symbolize the tension of desire.

The triumph of love over war was a favourite theme of Renaissance art. But in Gherardo's painting, Love is defeated by Chastity, whose shield breaks Cupid's arrow and whose chain will bind him.

The emblematic meaning of the **ARROW** is penetration – by light, by death, by love (human or divine), or by perception. Arrows appear as sun symbols and are the piercingly sweet darts of love. Phallic symbolism is prominent in Hinduism. Arrows can also stand for the wrath of Allah, Christian martyrdom and death, especially by lightning or by swift diseases like the plague. Bundled or broken (as in Native American symbolism), they represent peace. In shamanism, feathered arrows are an ascension symbol.

Beyond its obvious aggressive-protective function, the **SWORD** is an important symbol of authority, justice, intellect and light. One explanation for its unusually rich symbolism is that the arcane skills of sword-making meant that swords stronger, sharper and better balanced than others were credited with supernatural powers. Hence the frequent appearance of the sword as an emblem of magic and the many legends of magic swords, such as the Arthurian Excalibur, which can only be drawn by a man of exceptional virtue and strength – spiritual and physical.

Cults of the sword, particularly in Japan and in religious rituals of the medieval Crusades, gave it a ceremonial as well as a military role, especially in the conferring of knighthoods. A sword (in fable drawn from the tail of an eight-headed dragon) is one of the Three Treasures of the Japanese Emperor. In art, the sword is the attribute of justice, constancy, fortitude and wrath personified – and of St Paul who called the word of God "the sword of the spirit". The two-edged sword is specifically a symbol of divine wisdom or truth, notably in Revelation where it protrudes from the mouth of Christ (1:16). Because of a similarity of shape, there are close links here between the sword and the protruding tongue, which can also appear in art as an emblem of wisdom. Buddhism, too, uses the sword as an emblem of wisdom cutting through ignorance, and the Hindu god Vishnu is shown with a flaming sword of knowledge.

A Knight of the Round Table is shown in this 14th-century French illustration returning the sword Excalibur to the Lady of the Lake who had given it to Arthur as a symbol of his fitness to rule.

The flame-like shape of the two-edged sword also links it with purification, as in alchemy where the sword is an emblem of fire. Purity is implied by the biblical cherubim who, with a flaming sword, guard the way back to Eden (Genesis 3:24).

The sword laid between man and woman in bed in tales such as Tristram and Isolde is a symbol of self-discipline as well as separation. Dionysius, the tyrant of Syracuse, in legend suspended a sword by a hair above the head of an over-ambitious courtier, Damocles, as a reminder of the precarious nature of power.

As an emblem of justice the sword often appears with the scales. It is carried by the archangel Michael, and appears with retributive significance opposite the lily in paintings of the judgmental Christ. A broken sword symbolizes failure. In Chinese dream symbolism, a woman drawing a sword from water will have a son; and a sword falling into water presages a woman's death.

The oriental scimitar held by this 15th-century Mughal prince symbolizes his leading role as a warrior of the one true God of Islam.

Ark, Wheel and Chariot

The salvation and regeneration symbolism of an **ARK** or boat preserving the continuity of life from floodwaters is found in the mythology of peoples all around the world. Particularly noteworthy is the Epic of Gilgamesh from Mesopotamia. In Christian tradition the ark can stand for the Church (carrying saints and sinners), for Mary bearing her son, or for Christ as Redeemer. The Hebrew Ark of the Covenant, a chest of gilded acacia, symbolized the pledge of divine protection. In more secular symbolism the ark is the earth adrift in space.

However, of all artefacts designed for transport the **WHEEL** is supreme in symbolism – a solar image of cosmic momentum, ceaseless change and cyclic repetition. The Egyptians linked the revolving potter's wheel (the probable origin of the vehicular wheel) with the evolution of mankind itself. The development of ray-like spokes around 2000BC made the wheel a more convincing solar image and increased its sense of whirling momentum. With the advent of chariots and their enormous military impact, the wheel became a major symbol not only of the sun but also of power and dominion generally in Egypt, the Near East, India and Asia.

A motif with two crossing lines inside a circle (known as the wheel cross and later the gamma cross of Christianity) predates the invention of the wheel and also appears in America where wheels were not used before the arrival of the Spanish. This ideogram appears to be a symbol of totality (the circle) and the divisions of space. Wheel and space symbols are sometimes hard to disentangle.

Noah's Ark, depicted in this 16th-century Turkish manuscript, shows the womb-like symbolism of boats as protectors of life.

Gods specifically linked with the wheel are usually solar or all-powerful – Asshur, Shamash and Baal in the Near East; Zeus, Apollo and Dionysus in Greece; Vishnu-Surya in India. Blazing wheels were once bowled down hills at the June solstice to encourage the chariot of the sun to keep rolling over the horizon and

This Tibetan prayer-wheel draws on Buddhist and Hindu symbolism linking the turning wheel with the cycles of birth, death and rebirth, and human destiny.

reappearing next day. In the extraordinary biblical visions of the prophet Ezekiel, wheels appear again and again as symbols of Jehovah's divine omnipotence, the inexorability of his moral laws, and the undeviating path followed by his angels.

The symbolism of the rotating wheel as an unyielding law of life dominates much of the iconography of Buddhism. The Wheel of Existence carries humanity from one incarnation to another in ceaseless cycles as long as it clings to illusion. Only the Wheel of Law and Doctrine can crush illusion. The Buddha is its unmoving centre. Taoism uses the axle of the wheel as a symbol of the sage who has reached the still heart of the turning world. Wheel symbolism influenced the choice of the lotus and rose as the dominant symbolic flowers of East and West. The turning chakras that control the flow of spiritual energy in Tantric Buddhism are often shown as lotus wheels; and the rose windows of cathedrals are wheel symbols of spiritual evolution.

CHARIOTS OF FIRE

The chariot in ancient iconography is a dynamic symbol of rulership, widely used to illustrate the mastery and mobility of gods and heroes, or the spiritual authority of religious and allegorical figures. Its triumphal symbolism probably owes much to the shock force of chariot-riding warriors who spread out from central Asia from the 2nd millennium BC. Hindu mystics (later supported by psychologists such as Jung) saw charioteering as a symbol of the Self: the charioteer (thought) uses the reins (willpower and intelligence) to master the steeds (life force) that pull the chariot (the body). In moral allegory, the chariot thus became an image of the triumphant journey of the spirit, a symbolism used by the makers of the film *Chariots of Fire*. A fiery chariot carried the prophet Elijah to heaven (2 Kings 2:11). Wheel symbolism fitted aptly to the chariots of sun gods such as Helios or moon goddesses such as Diana. Equally, the sound of rumbling wheels suggested the chariots of Thor and other thunder gods. Gods or allegorical figures are more often identified by the specific symbolism of the creatures that draw their chariots. Thus Chastity is drawn by unicorns, Eternity by angels, Death by black oxen and Fame by elephants.

In this 14th-century illumination from the Roman de la Rose, *the power of Venus is symbolized by her chariot, drawn by six white doves, the traditional attributes of love goddeses.*

Clothes and Accessories

The transforming effect of **CLOTHES** has always given them considerable emblematic power. For example, the **CLOAK**'s symbolism of metamorphosis and concealment is related to the swiftness with which a cloak can change or hide the form. Magic cloaks appear often in Teutonic and Celtic legends, particularly those of Ireland; they are associated with special powers, including invisibility and forgetfulness. Alternatively, the cloak stands for intrigue – the cloak-and-dagger world of espionage.

Helmets like this elaborate Japanese one could both protect and symbolize the invisible power of thought.

The **HELMET** was also associated with invisible power, magic helmets assisting heroes such as Perseus who used one to slay the Gorgon Medusa. Here, the symbolic link is with the intellect. **CAPS** appear frequently in ancient

---

GIRDLES OF HONOUR

In the older sense of a belt or sash, the girdle acquired a varied symbolism because it was used not only to hold garments together (making it an emblem of female chastity) but also to carry weapons, provisions, money and tools. In Rome, laying aside the girdle implied retirement from military service – the opposite of warriors "girding up their loins". Its sexual symbolism ranged from marital fidelity (a girdle of wool given by Romans to their brides) to seductiveness (the magic girdle of the goddess Aphrodite, said to make its wearer irresistible to men). Magic girdles appear in mythology as emblems of strength; the belt of Thor doubled the power of his muscles. Deriving from the ornate girdles of chivalry, ceremonial girdles were awarded as emblems of honour in England; hence the "belted earl". The rope girdles of monks allude to the binding and scourging of Christ. Circle symbolism makes the Hindu girdle an emblem of the cycles of time.

The Franciscan girdle has three knots signifying obedience to Christ and the vows of poverty and chastity laid down by St Francis of Assisi, depicted in this 13th-century painting.

A felt Phrygian cap, worn by freemen in ancient Greece, became a French symbol of liberty, as shown in Delacroix's Liberty Leading the People.

iconography, again associated with wisdom and high status, especially when tall and conical. The pointed cap of the wizard symbolizes supernatural power. The dunce's cap and the jester's cap with its flopping bells are mocking inversions of this tradition. The **TURBAN** is a traditional emblem of the Islamic faithful and a symbol of personal honour for Sikhs.

The **GLOVE** was a powerful symbol of the executive hand itself, often used as a pledge of action in days when gloves were more widely worn, especially by people of rank. Removing the right glove acknowledged submission to an overlord and showed no threat was intended to him. The custom of throwing down a glove as a challenge (later, slapping someone in the face with a glove) goes back to medieval trials by battle. Defendants who lost cases deposited a folded glove as security that they would carry out the court order. Gloves were also used by jousting knights as love pledges.

Among other accessories, extensive symbolism surrounds the **RING**. Circle symbolism makes it an emblem of completion, strength and protection, and of continuity – all of which help to give significance to engagement and wedding rings. The oldest surviving rings (from Egypt) are signets bearing either personal seals or amulets, usually in the form of a scarab beetle symbolizing eternal life. Thus from the earliest times the ring has been an emblem of authority or delegated authority, of occult protective power and of a personal pledge. The Pope's Fisherman's Ring (showing Peter drawing in a net), broken at his death, is the supreme Roman Catholic seal. The plain gold nun's ring is a binding symbol of her "marriage" to Christ. Rings are commonly associated with magical force or hidden treasure in many legends – a theme which goes back to the belief that Solomon's ring was the source of his supernatural powers and wisdom.

The scarab beetle mounted on this pharaonic bracelet was an ancient Egyptian solar symbol used on funerary rings and other accessories to signify continuity.

Masks

Masks are a dramatic means of projecting symbolism in religion, ritual and theatre. Their primary role in the ancient world was to represent a supernatural force or even to transform their shaman wearers into the spirits their masks depicted. The earliest animal masks appear to have been used to capture the spirit of a hunted animal and thus prevent it from harming the wearer. Later primitive masks had totemic significance, identifying the tribe with a particular ancestral spirit whose vital force the mask attempted to capture so that it could then be used to protect the tribe, frighten its enemies, exorcise demons or diseases, expel the lingering spirits of the dead, or provide a focus for worship. Members of the Iroquois False Face society were exorcizers of disease demons, masked to symbolize the baleful twin brother of the creator god.

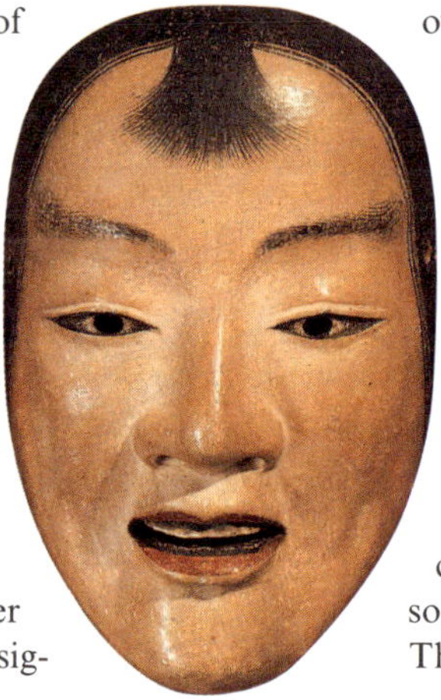

In the highly formal No theatre of Japan, masks are used with stylized colour symbolism – red for virtue, white for corruption, black for villainy – to display the unchanging forces that operate either at a supernatural level or in the human mind and heart.

Masks were also used in Oceanic, African and Native American initiation ceremonies to mark the transition from a childish to an adult appearance. In the Aleutian Islands in the north Pacific, a death mask was used in ritual as a way of confronting and also overcoming the the primal fear of death. Burial masks representing dead notables were widely used not merely to shield their decaying faces, as in the golden masks of Mycenae, but also to ensure that their souls, released at death, could eventually find their way back to their bodies. This was a particular point of concern in Egyptian and some other funerary rites.

The tragic and comic masks worn to identify different characters in ancient Greek drama developed from the religious masks used to act out myths or to symbolize the presence of divinities, particularly in the fertility cult of Dionysus. Asian demon-frightening masks (which survive today in processional dragon and lion dances) may similarly have been the origin of the masks later used in the Japanese No theatre. The mask can also, more obviously, symbolize concealment or illusion. In Indian tradition the mask is *maya* – the world as a delusion projected by the individual who has not understood the divine *maya* or Mask of God. In Western art, the mask is an attribute of deceit personified, and of vice and night.

The sumptuous Chinese processional mask opposite derives from ancient masks that were designed to terrify demonic spirits by presenting a mirror image of their own ferocity.

Emblems of Power

The supreme and most familiar emblem of spiritual or temporal authority is the **CROWN**, a form of headdress designed to identify, glorify or consecrate chosen individuals. Crowns originated as simple **WREATHS** which drew on the celestial symbolism of the circle (representing perfection) and the ring (continuity). Rulers awarded themselves more distinguished wreaths of gold or roses and diadems of cloth set with jewels, or ornate helmets with horns, jewels or feathers, and these various forms were gradually combined into metalled and jewelled crowns with increasingly elaborate significance. Christ's mocking crown of thorns (which became the crown of martyrs) had ancient precedents in the crowning of sacrificial victims as a mark of consecration.

A model displays a shamanic bear-claw crown and staff from America's northwest coast. Both these power symbols could imply spiritual rather than temporal authority and had protective meaning in many cultures, depending upon the animals or figures featured in their design.

Rulers traditionally symbolized their authority by seating themselves on **THRONES**. The diamond throne is a Buddhist emblem of the centre. Steps or a dais (elevation) and canopy (heavenly protection) often support the power symbolism of the seat itself. Jewels, precious metals and effigies of solar creatures, such as the lion or peacock, are decorative features that contribute their own symbolism of glory to the throne. Punitive emblems of state power include the Roman **FASCES**, an axe bundled in rods from which the axe head projected. For Mussolini, the fasces provided a coercive symbol for the political aims of Fascism.

In Egypt, the **FLAIL**, more a threshing tool than a weapon of chastisement, was an emblem of rulership, judgment and also fertility. All of this symbolism attaches also to the **WHIP**. The Roman Lupercalia festival featured young priests running about striking women with goatskin thongs to drive out sterility. Christ symbolized his spiritual authority by using a whip to chase money-changers from the Temple. Modern use of the whip in Islam is often more symbolic than physically punishing. A similar authority emblem to the flail in Africa, China and India is the **FLY WHISK**.

The **ROD** or **WAND** was an ancient emblem of supernatural power, symbolically associated with the potency of the tree or

Victors at the ancient Olympic games wore different wreaths honouring specific gods: an olive wreath for Zeus, Isthmian pine for Poseidon and the Pythian laurel wreath depicted here for Apollo.

branch, the phallus, the snake and the hand or pointing finger. A more specialized symbolism attaches to the **CADUCEUS**, a rod entwined by snakes. In legend the ambassadorial staff of Mercury, it came to be used as a protective emblem by messengers on political or commercial business. The stick with entwined serpents combined an axial pole suggesting phallic power with a double spiral formed by the snakes, suggesting cosmic energy, duality and the union of opposites. Its association with medicine comes from a symbolic link between the snake and rejuvenation.

This image from a 17th-century German alchemical manuscript shows an adept holding the double sceptre of the Secret Fire.

The ruler's **SCEPTRE**, like the **STAFF**, rod and **CROZIER** originated as a masculine fertility symbol. It often implies royal or spiritual power to administer justice, including punishment. Thus the pharaonic sceptre of Egypt was topped by the head of the violent god Set. Other sceptres are more specifically linked with the creative-destructive force of the thunderbolt – in particular the diamond sceptre or *vajra* of Hindu and Buddhist tradition and the Tibetan *dorje*. They symbolize both spiritual dominion and compassionate wisdom. Universal authority is symbolized by a spherical top, as in the sceptre of British monarchs with orb and cross. The **GLOBE** or **ORB** is a power emblem of gods or imperial rulers dating from at least the Roman Empire. Sharing with the sphere the symbolism of totality, it is also an attribute in art of figures representing universal qualities from truth, fame and fortune to justice, philosophy and the liberal arts.

In this portrait of Tsar Alexis of Russia (1629–76) the orb surmounted by a cross held in his left hand represents the dominion of Christ, the sceptre his own temporal authority.

Instruments of Music

MUSIC was linked with the origin of life itself in some traditions, notably in India where sound is regarded in Hindu doctrine as the primordial vibration of divine energy. From this comes the legend of Krishna's **FLUTE**, which reputedly brought the world into existence.

Primitive music, based on rhythm and imitations of the sounds of animals and the natural world, was essentially an attempt to communicate with the spirit world. With the development of more sophisticated instruments and harmonics, music became a symbol of cosmic order. It was associated in China and in Greece with number symbolism, and with the planets in the concept of "the harmony of the spheres". Plato believed that the cosmos formed a musical scale and number, and that the planets would create a divine harmony by moving at different speeds, just as musical pitch changed when strings of different lengths were vibrated. Yin or yang qualities were allocated in the semitones of the earliest Chinese "octave", music thus becoming a symbol of the vital duality holding together disparate things. In art, musicians or musical instruments often symbolize peace or love.

In many religions, the **BELL** is the divine voice that proclaims the truth, especially in Buddhist, Hindu, Islamic and Christian tradition. Its sound was a repercussion of the power of the godhead in Islamic and Hindu thought, and of cosmic harmony in China where the bell also stood for obedience. Small tinkling bells can represent happiness, and also sexual pleasure, as in Greek rites where they were associated with Priapus. Conversely, they were worn on Hebrew dresses as a sign of virginity. The bell is a passive, feminine principle, its shape a link with the celestial vault, its clapper symbolizing the tongue of the preacher. It was regarded as protective, warding off or exercising evil. More generally, it marks the passing of time, proclaims good news such as weddings or victories (the United States'

The music of the bells played by a deity and his companion in this 17th-century Tibetan bronze symbolizes the need to hear and obey the laws of the Buddha.

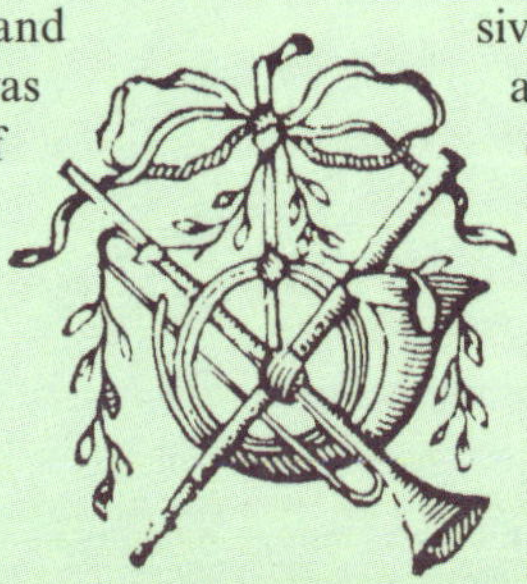

In art, the trumpet symbolizes fame, and is blown by the seven angels of the Last Judgment. Trumpets announced news brought by heralds, and also introduced knights in jousting.

Liberty Bell) or warns of danger. Because it tolls for death, it can symbolize human mortality.

Of all musical instruments, the **DRUM** is the most primeval means of communication, its percussive sound travelling to the heart and, by extension, suggesting the ability to communicate with supernatural forces. It symbolizes the creative-destructive power of Shiva, Kali and Indra, the Buddhist voice of the Law, the Chinese voice of heaven, the universal voice of cosmic energy. The ancient use of the drum to inspire warriors draws on the instrument's association with thunder as a symbol of destructive force. Drumming was widely used to achieve states of ecstasy in which spirits were invoked or shamans could move beyond the material plane.

The **TRUMPET** is the most portentous musical instrument – a traditional way to mark significant events, momentous news or violent action – hence the boastful meaning of "blowing your own trumpet". In Christian art, trumpets announce the Last Judgment and the Day of Wrath. The Romans popularized the shock effect of blowing trumpets before cavalry charges, as well as at ritualistic and state ceremonies.

By contrast, the **LYRE** symbolizes divine harmony, the vibration of the cosmos, musical inspiration and divination. It is the musical instrument most plausibly linked with classical mythology and, in particular, with Orpheus, whose music charmed wild beasts. The seven-stringed lyre denoted the seven planets; a 12-stringed version represented the signs of the zodiac. In myth, the lyre was invented by Hermes who gave it to Apollo, whose attribute it became. The **LUTE**, too, has many symbolic meanings. In China, it was an attribute of the scholar and of harmony – in marriage as well as in government. A popular emblem of the lover in Renaissance art, the lute symbolizes music and hearing. Lutes or mandolins with broken strings appear in still-lifes as symbols of discord.

The lyre symbolizes poetry and was the instrument of Terpischore, Greek muse of dance and song. Here, in a 15th-century psalter painted by Fra Angelico, the player is King David.

Patterns and Graphics

Although most symbols represent features of the visible universe, some of the most compelling rely only on pattern or colour, line or geometric shape. The grandest concepts are often represented by the simplest graphics. For example, the centre and origin of life, the idea of pure being, is widely repesented as a point – as in the concept of the Tao, which is "nought but infinity ... neither this nor that". This ancient symbolism of infinitely compressed energy, widespread in mystical writing, comes close to the theories of modern physics. Similarly, in Chinese art, eternity was symbolized in non-material form as a hole.

Many shapes or lines are not as abstract as they look. We respond to them subconsciously because they are based on ancient human responses to the natural world. The symbolic power of the circle, star, cross, spiral or swastika all depend on cosmic dynamics, directions of space or natural forms and rhythms. The symbolism of colours (red as "vital" or white as "pure"), our feeling that squares and cubes convey stability, and the calming effect of certain patterns are all deeply embedded in the human psyche.

Patterns can have exact meanings, as in the Sumerian writing tablet above, or symbolic ones, as in the antique Kashmiri carpet opposite. Islamic arabesques originally symbolized a complex journey toward sublime clarity, forming a kind of contemplative visual incantation.

Lines of Force

The **SWASTIKA**, an ideogram representing cosmic dynamism and creative energy, is one of the most ancient and widespread of all linear symbols. Named from the Sanskrit *su* "well", and *asti* "being", its traditional significance was always positive. The swastika itself is an equal-armed cross with the end of each arm turned at a right angle to give it whirling momentum.

A ponderous reverse swastika, often tilted to add dynamism, was used by the Nazi Party. An ancient and positive symbol of cosmic regeneration was transformed into an political emblem of brute force.

Pictorially it can suggest a solar wheel with light trailing from each turning spoke, and its appearance in many primitive cults was linked with sun or sky gods, particularly Indo-Iranian. It can rotate in either direction. The swastika with the top bar turned to the left – a Buddhist symbol of the cyclic round of existence – is sometimes, but not always, identified with the principle of male energy and was an emblem used by Charlemagne. The reversed swastika was linked with female generative power in upper Mesopotamia and appears on the pubis of the great Semitic goddess Ishtar. It is also a yin symbol in China.

The swastika's essential meaning of life force, solar power and cyclic regeneration is often extended to signify the Supreme Being, notably in Jainism. It appears on the footprint or breast of the Buddha (unmoving heart of the Wheel of Becoming) and is also a sign of Christ in catacomb inscriptions, and of Vedic, Hindu and Greek gods.

The winged disk on a swastika was widely used as a symbol of solar energy, particularly in Egypt and Babylonia. Apart from its rotative force, the swastika's other notable graphic feature is that its four arms divide space into quarters; the swastika therefore has associations with the four wind gods, the four seasons, or the four cardinal points.

Just before World War I, anti-Semitic groups in Germany and Austria began using the swastika as an emblem of "Aryan" racial purity. Adolf Hitler, master of mass psychology, recognized its dynamism as a party emblem and put it on the Nazi banner in August 1920. Nazi use of the swastika's power symbolism made it one of the most infamously successful emblems of the 20th century.

The Nazis also made use of another ancient linear sign of power, the **ZIGZAG**, based on lightning. A double zigzag became the insignia of the SS, the Nazi elite corps.

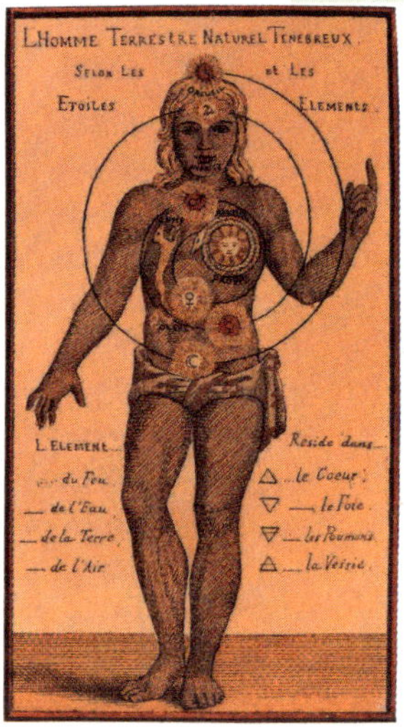

The cosmic symbolism of the spiral is used here to chart centres of psychic energy along a power path of elemental and astrological influences.

THE POWER OF THE SPIRAL

Spiral tattoos on the face of the 19th-century Maori chief Tamati Waka Nene symbolize the life force that drives the unfolding fern frond.

From the earliest times, the spiral has been a dynamic symbol of life force, cosmic and microcosmic. Spiral forms are seen in nature from celestial galaxies to whirlwinds and whirlpools, from coiled serpents or conical shells to human fingertips – and (as science has discovered) to the double-helix structure of DNA at the heart of every cell.

In art, spirals are one of the most common of all decorative motifs, ranging from Celtic double spirals in northern Europe or the volutes on Roman capitals, to the whorls in Maori carving and tattooing in the South Pacific. Maori whorls, which have sexual symbolism, are based on ferns and show the close links between spiral motifs and natural phenomena.

Carved on megaliths, spirals suggest a labyrinthine journey to the afterlife, and perhaps a return. Spiralling snakes on the caduceus – and double spirals in general – suggest a balance of opposing principles – the meaning of the yin–yang motif, which is itself a form of double spiral.

Vortex forces in wind, water or fire suggest ascent, descent or the rotating energy that drives the cosmos. By adding wheeling momentum to a circular form, the spiral also symbolizes time, the cyclic rhythms of the seasons and of birth and death, the waning and waxing of the moon, and the sun. Like the yogic "serpent" at the base of the spine, the springlike coil of a spiral suggests latent power. The uncoiling spiral is phallic and male, the involuted spiral is female, making the double spiral also a fertility symbol.

The spiral as an open and flowing line suggests extension, evolution and continuity, uninterrupted concentric and centripetal movement, the very rhythm of breathing and of life itself.

The Cross

In religion and art, the cross is the richest and most enduring of geometric symbols, taking many forms and meanings throughout history. It is both the emblem of the Christian faith and a more ancient and universal image of the cosmos reduced to its simplest terms – two intersecting lines making four points of direction. These stood for the four cardinal points and the four rain-bearing winds (notably in pre-Columbian America where the cross was often a fertility emblem of life and elemental energy), the four phases of the moon (Babylonia), and the four great gods of the elements (Syria).

The Maltese Cross, emblem of the Order of St John, is based on old Assyrian symbols. Its dart-like wings give it eight directional points.

The arms of the cross could be multiplied to six (as in Chaldea and Israel) or eight. In China, a cross within a square represented the earth and stability. In India, the cross was the Hindu emblem of the fire sticks of Agni; a cross within a circle, the Buddhist wheel of life; or, with arms extending beyond the circle, divine energy. The swastika – an ancient emblem of cosmic energy – was a cross given momentum by turning the ends of the arms.

The cross was also a summary of the Tree of Life; medieval Christians believed that Christ's cross was constructed from the Tree of Knowledge (the cause of the Fall) and so the cross gained symbolism as the instrument of human redemption. The vertical axis of the cross has ascensional meaning while the horizontal axis stands for earthly life – in Hindu and Buddhist terms, an image of higher and lower states of being. Another symbol of totality is the cross formed by a man standing with arms outstretched – Man as microcosm. More generally, the cross is associated with duality and union, conjunction and, in Jungian psychology, a kindling energy. Widespread veneration of the cross by peoples who knew nothing of Christianity puzzled early

The diagonal St Andrew's Cross was so named because Christian legend said Andrew chose martyrdom on it because he felt unworthy to die on the vertical cross of Christ.

The ankh – a cross surmounted by a loop – was used in ancient Egyptian funerary motifs like this one at Edfu to symbolize immortal life. In the 1st century AD *it was adopted into Christianity by the Coptic Church in Egypt.*

missionaries, particularly in North and Central America; in Mexico the cross was an attribute of the wind and rain gods, Quetzalcoatl and Tlaloc. Aztec images of sacrificial crucifixions have also been found. The mark of the cross in Africa could signify protection, cosmic unity, destiny or (in a circle) sovereignty. In Scandinavia, runic crosses marking boundaries and important graves may have represented the fertilizing power of the god Thor's hammer. The form of the Celtic cross, incorporating a circle at the centre of the crossbar, appears to synthesize Christian and pagan cosmic symbolism.

In the Roman, Persian and Jewish world, the crucifixion cross was the brutal and humiliating instrument of execution for non-citizens such as slaves, pirates and foreign political agitators or other criminals. Thus, at the time of Christ's death, it hardly seemed an emblem likely to make many converts. Fear of ridicule as well as persecution probably influenced the various forms of *crux dissimulata* (anchor, axe, swastika or trident) used by early Christians as secret cross emblems. Even after the Emperor Constantine's conversion, the cross remained for some centuries an emblem of faith secondary to a wheel-like monogram based on the first two Greek letters in the name Christ, Chi-Rho. The cross became dominant as Christianity spread because it could inherit older cross traditions and give them profound new meaning – redemption through Christ's self-sacrifice.

In art, representations of the crucifixion with an impassive Christ gradually gave way to powerful images of his agony, which culminate in Grünewald's Isenheim altarpiece (1515). By contrast, the plain cross became a consoling emblem of human suffering transcended. The Latin Cross (*crux immissa*), with a transverse bar below the top of the upright, is the most common crucifixion symbol, although it is not certain that Jesus died on such a cross. Some think a tau cross, or *crux commissa*, was used.

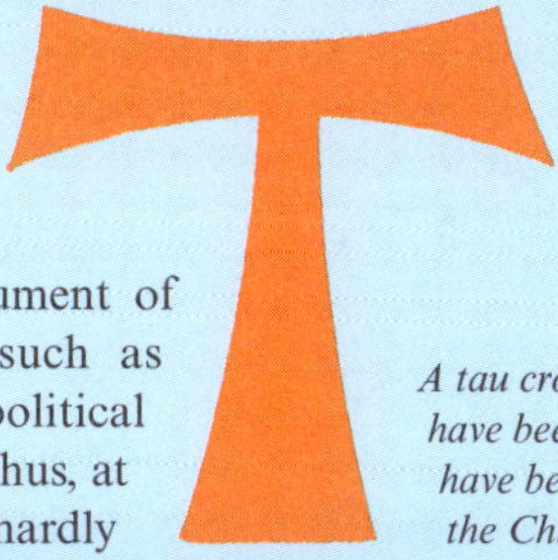

A tau cross with top horizontal bar may have been the cross of Christ. These crosses have been found on some early graves of the Christian era.

The Circle

The ouroboros – a snake swallowing its tail – symbolizes cyclic time, eternity and the indivisible, self-sustaining character of Nature.

The circle is the only geometric shape without divisions and alike at all points. Hence, perhaps, its symbolism of perfection, completeness and unity. As a form potentially without beginning or end, it is the most important and universal of all geometric symbols in mystical thought. And because it is implicit in other important symbols, including the wheel, disk, ring, clock, sun, moon, ouroboros and zodiac, its general symbolism is hardly less significant. To the ancients, the observed cosmos presented itself inescapably as circular – not only the planets themselves, including the presumed flat disk of the earth circled by waters, but also their cyclical movements and the recurring cycles of the seasons. Circles had protective as well as celestial significance, notably in the Celtic world – and they still do have this in the folklore of fairy rings and flying saucers. They also stand for inclusive harmony, as in the Arthurian Round Table or the "charmed circle" of acquaintanceship widely used in modern idiom. Interlocking circles (as in the modern Olympic emblem) are another symbol of union.

Dynamism is added to the circle in the many images of disks with rays, wings or flames found in religious iconography, notably Sumerian, Egyptian and Mexican. They symbolize solar power or creative and fertilizing cosmic forces. Concentric circles can stand for celestial hierarchies (as in the choirs of angels symbolizing heaven in Renaissance art), levels in the afterworld or, in Zen Buddhism, stages of spiritual development. Three circles can stand for the Christian divine Trinity but also for the divisions of time, the elements, the seasons or the movement of the sun and the phases of the moon. The circle can be masculine (as the sun) but also feminine (as the maternal womb). A circle (female) over a cross (male) is a symbol of union in Egypt, also known in northern Europe, the Middle East and China. The Chinese yin–yang symbol of male and female interdependence uses two colours within a circle,

Sky symbolism and belief in celestial power underlies ancient architecture throughout the world. Stonehenge consisted of 30 upright stones, forming a circle 30m (100ft) across.

divided by an S-shaped curve, each including a smaller circle of the opposing colour. The circle combined with the square is a Jungian archetypal symbol of the relationship between the psyche or self (circle) and the body or material reality (square). This interpretation is supported by Buddhist mandalas in which squares inside circles represent the passage from material to spiritual planes. In Western and Eastern thought the circle enclosing a square stands for heaven enclosing earth. Circular domes, vaults or cupolas incorporate the celestial symbolism of the rounded decoration in Romanesque churches or pagan temples into architecture based on the square, cross or rectangle. "Squaring the circle" (the geometrically impossible task of forming a circle from a series of squares) was a Renaissance and alchemical allegory of the difficulty of constructing divine perfection with earthly materials.

The Buddhist Wheel of the Law is an image of the phenomenal world, held within the cosmic circumference, inexorably changing and repeating itself.

MYSTIC RITES OF CIRCUMAMBULATION

In societies throughout the world, the ritual of walking around a sacred object, often an altar, pole, stone or other axial symbol, both defines and sanctifies a space. By making a circuit, the worshipper imitates solar and astral cycles, and pays homage to celestial forces. Like circular dancing, this kind of circumambulation draws on the ancient protective and cosmic power symbolism of the circle. In a celebrated example at Mecca, Islamic pilgrims make seven circuits of the Kaaba (sacred cube) and kiss the Black Stone at one corner. The Kaaba contains a meteorite said to have been given to Abraham by the archangel Gabriel as a divine mark of his spiritual authority. Buddhist circumambulation of a temple is also intended to place the worshipper in tune with cosmic rhythms and symbolizes a gradual progression toward self-knowledge and enlightenment. In both Buddhist and Hindu Pradakshina, the direction of circumambulation is clockwise, following the apparent clockwise path of the sun around the northern hemisphere. Muslims at Mecca walk counterclockwise, imitating the polar wheel of the stars.

The Kaaba, a cube-shaped structure at the heart of Mecca, symbolizes for Muslims the spiritual centre of the world – the origin of civilization, stability, totality and perfection.

Shapes and Signs

The Chi-Rho monogram is formed by combining the two initial Greek letters of the word Christ. It was believed to put one under the protection of Christ.

STAR shapes are among the most powerful of all graphic symbols. The five-pointed pentagram and six-pointed hexagram (drawn with internal lines connecting each point) have mystic associations. The four-pointed star is the sun star of Shamash, the Mesopotamian solar god. The five-pointed star was the Sumerian emblem of Ishtar in her warrior aspect as the morning star. As an emblem of ascendancy, it is the star that accompanies the crescent in Islamic symbolism, and the star most widely used on flags generally and in military and police insignia today. It is also the most common form of Bethlehem star or birth star. In Freemasonry, the five-pointed "blazing star" symbolizes the mystic centre and regeneration. The six-pointed star is the Star of David, the Pole Star, and sometimes appears as a birth star. The Gnostic mystic star has seven points. The eight-pointed star, linked with creation, fertility and sex, was the emblem of Ishtar as the evening star, and later of Venus. This is an alternative form of Bethlehem star.

A dream of Constantine the Great led to the sign known as the **CHI-RHO** symbol becoming a dominant Christian emblem for some centuries after Constantine made Christianity the official religion of the Roman Empire. The Chi-Rho displaced the eagle on the Roman standard when Constantine came to power by defeating Maxentius in 312AD. According to his biographer Eusebius (4th century AD), Constantine's final conversion to Christianity followed a dream in which he saw the Chi-Rho sign superimposed on the sun. What this suggests is that Constantine in effect identified Christ as a new incarnation of the sun. The sign was not new, for the Greek word for "auspicious", *chrestos*, also began with chi and rho, and a similar spoked-wheel emblem within a circle was earlier a Chaldean solar symbol. Both

This 12th-century Danish gilt image of Christ is enclosed by the sacred mandorla shape also used to symbolize the purity of the Virgin Mary, or other sanctified Christians borne to heaven.

HALO, NIMBUS AND AUREOLE

A circular radiance, the **HALO**, was widely used, especially by Western artists between the 6th and 15th centuries AD, to symbolize divinity or sanctity. In early art, gilders often formed haloes with painstaking care from paper-thin squares of beaten gold. The symbolic convention, originally based on the nimbus surrounding the sun's disk, was adapted from pagan images of sun gods or deified rulers, particularly from the iconography of Mithras, god of light, whose cult Christianity supplanted in the Roman Empire only after a long struggle. In the Eastern Orthodox Church, the halo is often bisected by a cross. The "floating ring" image of a halo, which often now appears in popular represenations, was a later form.

Buddhist spiritual authority is symbolized by a halo backing the head in sculpture, or by a cloudier radiance in paintings, as in this Chinese image of the Bodhisattva Avalokiteshvara.

A cloudier form of radiance, the **NIMBUS**, symbolizes divinity or, in some cases, spiritual power and energy. It takes more varied forms, such as a triangular nimbus for God or the Trinity, cruciform for Christ, square for a living person and hexagonal for allegorical figures. Although the nimbus is usually golden in paintings, a white radiance sometimes appears in Christian art; red is preferred in Indian iconography.

As the etymology of **AUREOLE** indicates (from medieval Latin *aureola corona*, "crown of gold"), it is a term most aptly applied in a specific sense to radiance shown as a crown formed by spokes or beams of light, sometimes surrounding the body as well as the head.

Chi-Rho (Christ) and IC (Jesus Christ) appear as Christian funerary monograms.

One of the most familiar symbolic shapes in Christian art is the **MANDORLA** – an almond-shaped aureole used by medieval Christian sculptors and painters to frame the figure of Christ and symbolize his supernatural status and his ascension to glory. With its vulva-like oval shape and the whiteness of its pressed juice, the almond (*mandorle* in Italian) had ancient associations with ideas of self-pollination and virgin birth. Graphically, it also resembles a flame, a symbol of spirituality. Another view is that the shape of the almond represents the duality of heaven and earth – depicted as two intersecting arcs. This explains why mandorlas usually enclose ascending figures, symbolizing not only their sanctity but also their transfiguration.

The arch symbolizes the vault of the sky. Initiates passing under an arch symbolically leave their former lives and are born again.

Labyrinth Patterns

The varied and often ambivalent symbolism of the **LABYRINTH** probably dates from the mysteries, terrors and protective advantages of the cave systems in which humans once dwelt. The earliest known artificial labyrinths, in Egypt and Etruria (central Italy), were built to keep the tombs of kings inviolate.

Early labyrinthine decorations on Greek houses took up this protective symbolism in motifs designed to confuse evil spirits. Remarkable plumbing conduits at the Minoan palace of Knossos may have been the origin of the legendary Cretan labyrinth in which Theseus killed the Minotaur. The usual reading of this influential myth is that Theseus, who is a symbol of the saviour-hero, overcame the brutish aspects of his own character as well as the power of Minos. This meshes with the major religious and psychological meanings of passing through a labyrinth – that it represents an initiation, a symbolic return to the womb, a "death" leading to rebirth, the discovery of a spiritual centre, the laborious and often perplexing process of self-discovery. Many labyrinths are unicursal, having no traps but leading sinuously along a single path. These were often used in early temples as initiation routes or more widely for religious dances that imitated the weaving paths of the sun or planets. They reappeared in patterns on the floors of medieval Christian churches as "roads to Jerusalem" – paths symbolizing pilgrimage. At Chartres cathedral, France, penitents shuffled 650ft (200m) on their knees along such a circular maze within an area only 40ft (12m) in diameter.

Some of the ambivalent symbolism of the labyrinth is shared by **KNOTS.** In decoration, loose, interwoven knot patterns can represent infinity or longevity. Tight knots often symbolize union – as in the familiar Victorian custom of tying the wedding knot; and in art, the tying of a knot by Cupid in depictions of Venus and Mars denotes the ties of love. Union is also the symbolism of the knotted cord worn by Brahmins, binding them to Brahma in the same way as the thrice-knotted cord of the Franciscan friar binds him to his vows of poverty, celibacy and obedience.

Alternatively, tight knots can represent blockage and often had protective symbolism, based on the idea of frustrating evil spirits. Curious fishermen's superstitions in Northern Europe and Scotland attach magic significance to knots tied in handkerchiefs or cords, thought to influence the weather.

A stone knot, probably with protective symbolism, is a feature of this wall in an early Islamic palace. Muslims knotted their beards to baffle demons, but forbade knots in holy places such as the mosque at Mecca.

Labyrinth patterns, such as this splendid ceiling in the ducal palace at Mantua, give graphic form to the manifold and difficult choices of life. This was the symbolism of a labyrinth pattern used as a heraldic device by the Mantua house of Gonzaga, accompanied by the motto: "Perhaps yes, perhaps no." Labyrinths formed by garden hedges turn the dilemma into a game.

Geometric Forms and Patterns

The **PENTAGRAM** is an ancient geometric symbol of harmony, health and mystic powers – a five-pointed star with lines that cross to each point. When used in magic rituals, this sign is usually called the **PENTACLE**. The pentagram seems to have originated in Mesopotamia 4,000 years ago, probably as an astronomical plot of the movements of the planet Venus. It is thought to have been the figure used on the Seal of Solomon and was the official seal of Jerusalem *c.*300–*c.*150BC. In Greece, the Pythagoreans adopted it as an emblem of health and mystic harmony. From this point on, the pentagram steadily acquired occult meaning, medieval sorcerers associating it with Solomon's reputed powers over nature and the spirit world.

Magicians sometimes wore pentacle caps of fine linen to conjure up supernatural help. With one point upward and two down, the pentacle was the sign of white magic, the "Druid's foot". With one down and two up, it represented the "Goat's foot" and horns of the Devil – a characteristic symbolic inversion. The pentacle was also a Masonic aspirational symbol.

The **HEXAGRAM**, or Star of David, is sometimes identified with Solomon. It has two interlocking triangles, one inverted, symbolizing union in duality. Hexagram shapes appear in Indian mandalas as meditative images and, with mysterious significance, in Central American rock carvings. In alchemy, the hexagram symbolized the male/female dualities of fire and water, later the union of the four elements or the "fifth element" (the quintessence). In magic, the hexagram was associated with exorcism.

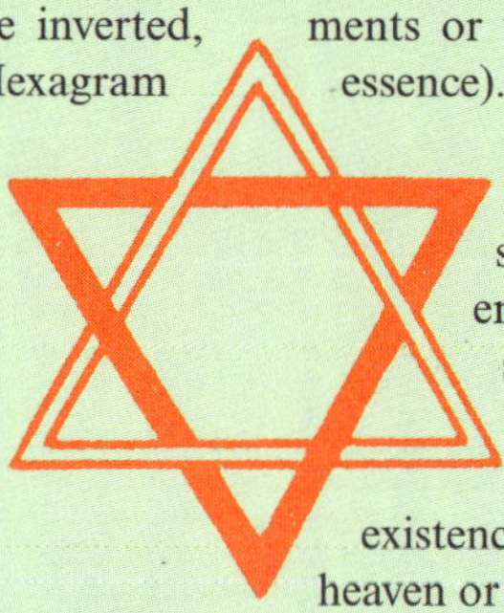

The hexagram is now more usually known as the Star of David, the Hebrew king who unified Judah and Israel. It is the emblem of the modern state of Israel.

The **OCTAGON** draws on the symbolism of the number eight, emblematic of renewal. Eight-sided forms were felt to mediate between the symbolism of the square, representing earthly existence, and the circle (standing for heaven or eternity).

The octagon symbolizes rebirth to eternal life in religious architecture, hence the design of the 5th-century Neonian Baptistry at Ravenna.

The triangular Trimurti emblem symbolizes the sacred Hindu grouping of Brahma, Vishnu and Shiva – the three cycles of creation, preservation and destruction.

The **TRIANGLE** is one of the most powerful and versatile geometric symbols. The equilateral triangle sitting on its base is a male and solar sign representing divinity, fire, life, the heart, ascent, prosperity, harmony and royalty. The reversed triangle, by association with the pubic triangle, is female and lunar, representing the great mother, water, fecundity, rain and heavenly grace. Male and female triangles meeting at their points signify sexual union. The triangle is the sign for God in several major religions.

The ancient sign for the earth was the **SQUARE**, particularly important in the symbol systems of India and China. Based on the order implied by the four directions of space, the square symbolized permanence, security, balance and the rational organization of space, as well as honesty, integrity and morality.

THE SERENE MANDALA

Mandala designs symbolize spiritual, cosmic or psychic order. Although Buddhist mandalas, particularly in the geometric form of the yantra, have become famous as aids in meditative exercises, ancient mandala forms in both Hinduism and Buddhism also had initiatory symbolism, orienting worshippers to a sacred space. They are attempts to provide an image of the supreme reality – of a spiritual wholeness that transcends the world of appearances. They symbolize progression toward a spiritual centre, either mentally or physically – as in the mandala structure of many temples or stupas. The striking feature of all mandala patterns is their careful balancing of visual elements, symbolizing a divine harmony beyond the confusion or disorder of the material world. To Jung, these patterns were archetypal symbols of the human longing for psychic integration. To others, the mandala represents a spiritual journey out of the self. The meaning of individual mandalas differs; some have figurative elements that invite contemplation of, for example, the specific virtues embodied by a particular Bodhisattva, often shown seated within a lotus.

This mandala depicts four doors and eight snake divinities within a mystic circle. The Sanskrit meaning of mandala *is "circle"; mandalas that use squares still have concentric structures.*

Colours

Colours in general are life-affirming symbols of illumination. Inevitably, **WHITE**, the absolute colour of light, became a symbol of purity, truth, innocence and the sacred or divine. Although it has some negative connotations – fear, cowardice, surrender, coldness, blankness and the pallor of death – white is the positive side of the black-white antithesis in all symbol systems. It is also the colour of initiation, the novice, neophyte or candidate (the Latin word for which means "shining white") and of rites of passage, including baptism, confirmation, marriage – through links between light and joy. As the colour of spirituality and sanctity, truth and revelation, it was worn by the Druids and other priestly classes in the pagan as well as the Christian world. With the same sacral meaning, white was also worn by sacrificial

THE ENERGY OF RED

In some early societies red was so linked with life that red ochre was painted on bodies to ensure resurrection. It is the active and masculine colour of fire, war, energy, aggression, danger, political revolution, impulse, emotion, passion, love, joy, festivity, vitality, health, strength and youth.

As the colour of arousal, it was also linked with sexuality – with the phallic god, Priapus in Greece, and with the "scarlet woman" of prostitution. In China, where it was the emblem of the Chou dynasty and of the south, it was the luckiest of all colours. Red on white could symbolize lost blood and the pallor of death, but the Asian red beauty spot is protective. In the Chinese theatre, red paint on an actor's face identifies him or her as a holy character. Calendars marking feasts and saints' days in red are the origin of the "red-letter" day.

Red is the emblematic colour of power and therefore of gods of war such as the Roman Mars, seen here with the goddess Juno.

Black Virgin icons appear to relate to positive pagan symbolism of black as the colour of the mothering and germinating earth.

victims. The white dove symbolizes peace, the white lily chastity.

BLACK has almost inescapable symbolism as the colour of negative forces and unhappy events. It stands for the darkness of death, ignorance, despair, sorrow and evil (whose Prince of Darkness is Satan), for inferior levels or stages (the underworld, primary dissolution in alchemy), and for ominous augury. In superstition – and in modern English idiom – black is synonymous with disaster: black cats, black days, black spots, black marks, black-balling. As the colour of mourning, it dramatizes loss and absence. As the colour of Christian and Muslim clerics, it signals renunciation of life's vanities. Black has also been an avenging colour in Islam, a tradition echoed by the Black September terrorists at the Munich Olympic games in 1972.

Yet in Egypt and some other ancient traditions, black had earth and maternal symbolism. The Hindu Kali and Durga can appear as black goddesses, suggesting the light-dark duality necessary to the continuation of life, as expressed by the black-and-white Chinese yin–yang symbol.

BLUE symbolizes infinity, eternity, truth, devotion, faith, purity, chastity, peace, spiritual and intellectual life – associations that appear in many ancient cultures and express a general feeling that blue, the colour of the sky, is the coolest, most detached and least "material" of all hues. The Virgin Mary and Christ are often shown wearing blue, and it is the attribute of sky gods. Blue is linked to mercy in Hebrew tradition and to wisdom in Buddhism. In folk traditions it stands in Europe for fidelity, in parts of China for scholarship and happy marriage. Still more recent are idiomatic links with melancholia, perhaps deriving from the twilight blues sung by African slaves in North America, and with pornography, from dimmed showings of explicit movies.

Krishna, the blue-skinned incarnation of Vishnu in the Hindu pantheon, is the god most easily identified in Indian art by his celestial colour.

The Green Lion of alchemy represents primary matter, which the illustration suggests can be transmuted to gold – symbolized by the sunflower it eats.

The colour with the most consistent symbolism is **GOLD**. Its solar associations and the prestige of the metal make it an emblem of glory, divinity, royalty, light and truth. **GREEN** is also a generally positive symbol, as is evident even in its use as the "go" colour in modern traffic signals. Green is universally associated with plant life and by extension with spring renewal, youth, freshness, fertility and hope. It has acquired powerful new symbolic resonance as a modern emblem of ecology.

Traditionally, the spiritual symbolism of green was most important in the Islamic world, where it was the sacred colour of the Prophet and of divine providence. It was the emblematic colour of the Ming dynasty in China, where green jade symbolized perfection, immortality or longevity, strength and magical powers. Green is also the symbolic colour of Ireland, the "Emerald Isle". Emerald green is a Christian emblem of faith, the reputed colour of the Holy Grail in Christianizing versions of the legend. Green sometimes appears as the colour of the Trinity, of revelation and, in early Christian art, of the Cross.

In the pagan world, green is more widely linked with water, rain and fertility, with gods and sprites of water, and with female deities, including the Roman goddess Venus. It is a female colour in Mali and in China. The Green Dragon of Chinese alchemy represented the yin principle, mercury and water

A secondary stream of symbolism is more ambivalent. Many traditions make a distinction between dark green (a Buddhist life colour) and the pale greenish tinge of death. The green of the god Osiris in Egyptian iconography symbolizes his role as god both of the dead and of new life. In English idiomatic usage, green represents immaturity but also the hues of envy and jealousy – the "green-eyed monster" of Iago's warning to Othello. Psychologically, green occupies a cool, neutral position in

Violet is associated with humility. This is the symbolism of violets bordering the Annunciation scene in this Flemish Book of Hours.

THE SYMBOLIC HUES OF YELLOW

Of all primary colours, yellow is the most ambivalent, swinging from positive to negative symbolism according to context and range of hue. Warm yellow shares the solar symbolism of gold. In China it is an emblem of royalty, merit and the centre. Yellow was the optimistic bridal colour of youth, virginity, happiness and fertility. Yet in the Chinese theatre, yellow make-up was the code for treachery. The symbolic connection between this colour and disloyalty appears to be widespread and may help to explain why Jews (for their supposed "betrayal" of Christ) had to wear yellow in medieval Europe and yellow crosses under Nazism. Links between yellow skin and fear or disease account for yellow corresponding to the colour of cowardice and quarantine. A yellow cross was painted on plague houses. In its negative aspect, yellow is also the colour of dying leaves; this is probably the basis of its association with death and the afterlife in some cultures. Yellow has the highest symbolic value in Buddhist countries through its link with the saffron robes of monks. This colour, previously worn by criminals, was chosen by Gautama Buddha as a symbol of renunciation.

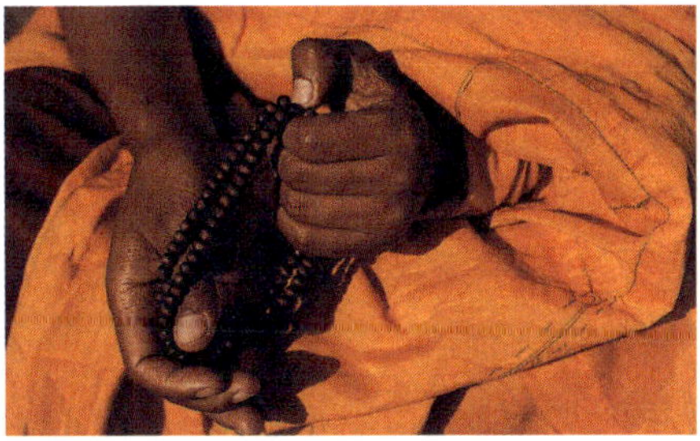

These beads are held by a monk wearing the saffron of Buddhism. This hue symbolizes humility and separation from materialist society.

the spectrum and is often regarded as a calming "therapeutic" hue – hence its use as the colour of pharmacy. Yet it is often linked with otherworldliness – the mystic colour of fairies and little people from outer space. Satan himself is sometimes represented as green. Perhaps this stems from the fact that green is not the skin-colour of healthy normality.

PURPLE denoted royalty, eminence and dignity in the ancient world. Its emblematic meaning was based on the high value of cloth dyed purple by the secretions of two species of molluscs, which was an expensive process. Purple was worn by high priests, magistrates and military leaders in the Roman world but was associated particularly with emperors. The children of Byzantine emperors were born in a room with purple drapes, hence the phrase "born in the purple". Cardinals are still said to be "raised to the purple" although their robes are actually red.

VIOLET is linked with temperance, moderation, spirituality and repentance, or a transition from active to passive, male to female, life to death. These interpretations are based on the mingling of red (passion, fire or earth) with blue (intellect, water or sky). Christ and Mary wear violet robes in some paintings of Passion scenes – the symbolism of violets in paintings of the Adoration, where they refer both to Mary's chastity and hidden virtue, and to the meekness of the Christ Child. Wreaths of violets were remembrance flowers in Rome and were worn at banquets to cool the brow.

Symbol Systems

Throughout history, humans have sought to explain the processes of nature and predict the apparently chaotic course of life. In this attempt, they have tried to marry spiritual and scientific approaches to knowledge, and have constructed complex systems of thought and belief which are often expressed in deeply symbolic form. These range from major predictive systems, such as astrology, the *I Ching* and the Tarot, to systems that rely more on pragmatism, such as the science of numbers or the pseudo-science of alchemy.

ASTROLOGY

Origins and development

Astrology is the divinatory system based on the interpretation of planetary configurations. Its earliest roots were in Babylonian civilization, and tablets dating back to the 7th century BC set out the influence on human affairs of four celestial deities – Shamash (the sun), Sin (the moon), Ishtar (the planet Venus) and Adad (the weather god). Over the centuries, these divinatory principles were transmitted through the Middle East, India and China, where they then developed independently, but it was not until the Hellenistic age that further significant advances were made in astrology. In the 2nd century AD Ptolemy named the constellations as we know them today, and improved methods of observation allowed Greek scholars to map the movement of the planets relative to fixed coordinates in the celestial sphere. The constellations were seen as a backdrop against which the apparent motions of the sun, moon and planets (five of which could be seen in ancient times) were charted. The sun and planets appeared to move (relative to the stars) within a narrow band of the sky, and this belt (or zodiac) was divided into twelve arcs of 30°, each corresponding to one of the twelve zodiacal signs. The signs were named after the most prominent constellations that (originally) fell within them.

In the development of astrology, celestial movements were matched with terrestrial cycles, and the zodiac acquired a system of symbols that denoted conditions on earth according to the part of the sky in which the sun appeared. For example, at the height of summer, Leo (the lion) signified the sun's fiery heat. This sign is followed by Virgo (the virgin), symbolic of the harvesting of seed for next year's planting. Libra (the scales) represented the equilibrium between summer and winter, the time of the autumnal equinox, when day and night are of equal length.

Even in Ptolemy's time, the Greeks noted that people appeared to fall into types of personality governed by the season of their birth. Over time, descriptions of twelve personality types evolved, which corresponded roughly to the signs of the zodiac. From these came the idea of individual horoscopes based on time of birth and various other more complex factors.

Signs of the zodiac

The twelve signs of the zodiac are arranged into four groups of three, and each group is associated with a particular element (fire, water, air or earth) and with a quality and

Zuccaro's elaborate painting on the ceiling of the Palazzo Farnese in Caprarola depicts the constellations in the night sky.

gender. The fire signs (Aries, Leo and Sagittarius) are linked to thrusting, energetic characteristics; the water signs (Pisces, Cancer and Scorpio) to emotional and intuitive traits; the air signs (Aquarius, Gemini and Libra) to logic and intellect; and the earth signs (Capricorn, Taurus and Virgo) to practicality and dependability. Fire and air signs are, in addition, seen as extroverted, and water and earth signs as introverted.

The qualities of the signs, or quadruplicities, are either cardinal, fixed or mutable, reflecting the three basic qualities of life – creation (cardinal), preservation (fixed) and destruction (mutable). Cardinal signs are active and initiate events; fixed signs are passive and hold events on course; mutable signs make way for change. The signs are also divided according to gender, alternating between "masculine" and "feminine". Finally, the twelve signs can be divided into six pairs or "polarities", each pair existing in balance.

Casting horoscopes

The influence on earth of the heavenly bodies was thought to depend on the positions of the planets within the signs; and because the planets were seen as the driving forces behind people and events on earth, they were closely linked with the gods. Each planet (ten in all, because the sun and moon are counted as planets for astrological purposes) has a symbol and is said to "rule" one or more of the signs. The positions of planets relative to one another, as seen from the earth, determine the interaction of the forces which the planets represent: the forces can work together when the planets are in approximately the same place in the sky (in conjunction), or against each other when the planets are separated by 90° (in opposition).

For the purpose of casting a horoscope, the sky – that is, the local rather than celestial sphere – is divided into twelve units or "houses" relative to the horizon. The houses are numbered rather than named, and give clues to aspects of an individual's life, such as relationships, health, work and creativity, depending upon which signs and planets are located within them.

The characteristics of each sign, the planetary influences and the areas defined by the houses, work together to produce a complex web of interrelationships. Science denies these connections and holds that the constellations which the ancients identified consist of heavenly bodies separated from each other by vast tracts of space, and so remote from our world that the possibility of their having any connection with our lives is out of the question. Astrology is thus seen as a pseudo-science, at best a crude forerunner of modern astronomy, although it still exerts a powerful hold on our consciousness.

I CHING

The *I Ching*, the Book of Changes, is one of the oldest methods of divination. Dating back to China between 1122 and 770BC, the book has evolved greatly since its initial compilation and its wisdom has been added to by sages thought to include Confucius. The *I Ching* reflects the philosophy of interconnectedness: its aim is less to determine the future, more to make the enquirer aware of possibilities.

Using the *I Ching*

Anyone consulting the *I Ching* formulates a question, then tosses a set of coins or yarrow sticks to generate a set of "lines" that may be broken (representing "no" or yin) or whole (representing "yes" or yang). Each permutation of three lines (trigram) or six lines (hexagram) is associated with a particular group of meanings, set out in the book.

The *I Ching* symbolizes the presence of opposites: night

and day, good and evil, fortune and misfortune, and so on. It recognizes that our perception of reality is based on these opposites, but acknowledges that the opposites are mutable – that nothing is permanent. In the trigrams, the two opposing combinations of three continuous lines (Ch'ien) and three broken lines (K'un) each takes on aspects of the other until the distinction between them disappears.

Originally, the divinatory system centred on the eight trigrams (combinations of three lines). These were later put together to form the sixty-four hexagrams, which were thought to represent all the basic human situations.

THE TAROT

The Tarot is a divinatory system based on the interpretation of a pack of 78 cards. The cards, which carry deeply symbolic images, are in effect two packs that have been brought into one: the *major arcana*, which consist of twenty-two trump cards, each one unique; and the *minor arcana*, which differ from modern playing cards only in that the court cards in each of the suits are four in number (king, queen, knight and page or princess) instead of three, and that the suits themselves are pentacles (or coins), cups, wands and swords.

Origins of the pack

The origins of the Tarot remain a mystery. Attempts have been made to trace it back variously to the ancient civilizations of Egypt, India and China; its introduction into Europe has been credited to both the Arabs and the Gypsies (Romanies). Another theory is that the *minor arcana* was based, in part at least, upon unknown sets of cards brought back by Venetian traders from the East some time prior to the 15th century, and associated with the Hindu god Vishnu. Vishnu is traditionally shown with four arms and holding the disc, lotus, club and conch which symbolize the divine powers of preservation (karma yoga), love (bhakti yoga), wisdom (gnana yoga) and inner realization (raja yoga). These four symbols may be the origin of the four suits of the *minor arcana*.

If this is the case, the cards of the *minor arcana* were intended not as playing cards but as allegories of the soul's journey along four parallel paths toward spiritual enlightenment. In the course of this journey the individual progresses through the stages represented by each numbered card and court card to the ultimate level of kingship. The *major arcana*, which probably also came to Venice from the East, may have been designed to show a more esoteric spiritual route in which the four paths of the *minor arcana* are integrated into one.

Developing meanings

How the two packs became combined into one is unclear, but the first recorded pack to resemble modern packs is believed to have been made for the Duke of Milan in 1415. From the early 15th century, the combined pack came to be used widely in France as well as in Italy, and eventually spread throughout Europe. In the course of time its rich original meanings became overlaid by its use as playing cards; and because the *major arcana* proved too complex for this purpose, it disappeared from what is now the modern playing pack.

There is a strong tradition that locates the Tarot's origins in the body of universal knowledge laid down by the Egyptian god Thoth for his disciples in magic. Inspired by this theory, a Paris wigmaker who called himself Etteila (his real name spelled in reverse) devised his own Tarot pack for divination purposes. This was taken up in the mid-19th century by Eliphas Lévi (the occult pseudonym of Alphonse Louis Constant) who extended Etteila's ideas into a complete system, based upon Egyptian images, and linked with the Cabbala.

Lévi's interpretation is based on suspect premises, but the Cabbalistic echoes of the Tarot are undeniable. For example, the twenty-two letters of the Hebrew alphabet correspond with the twenty-two *major arcana* cards of the Tarot; and the four suits of the minor arcana could be said to reflect the four Cabbalistic "worlds", the four steps by which God created the cosmos.

NUMBERS

For the ancients, numbers symbolized divine order and represented the cryptic keys to cosmic harmony. The mathematical philosophers of ancient Babylonia and Greece, and later, India, believed that the study of numbers could reveal the principles of creation and the laws of space and time. In the interplay of odd and even numbers the Greek philosopher Pythagoras (*c*.580–500BC) saw the workings of a dualistic universe of opposites – limit and unlimited, straight and curved, square and oblong. "All things are numbers," he said. In Hinduism numbers were the basis of the material universe. The Aztecs assigned to each fundamental number a god, a quality, a direction and a colour. Because numbers were used by the gods to regulate the world, each was thought to have a particular significance.

Numbers were also seen as fundamental in music, poetry, architecture and art. Jewish Cabbalist mystics in the 3rd century allocated number values to the letters of the Hebrew alphabet and used the system to reinterpret the Old Testament. This led to the later rise of numerology as a pseudo-science studying the occult influence of numbers on human affairs. Number superstition is often based on the traditional symbolism of numbers (such as mystic seven, unlucky 13).

The sequence one, two, three almost universally represented unity, duality and synthesis. In Pythagorean terms, one, two, three, four symbolized the flow from point to line to surface to solid. In Greece, odd numbers were masculine and active, even numbers feminine and passive. In China, odd numbers were yang, celestial, immutable and auspicious; even were yin, terrestrial, mutable and sometimes less auspicious. Numbers with archetypal significance ran from one to ten (or one to 12 in duodecimal systems). Higher numbers in which important archetypes reappear (17 in Islamic tradition; 40 in the Semitic world) often serve to reinforce number symbolism.

Twenty was a sacred number in Central America, associated with the sun god, and 21 was linked with wisdom in Hebrew tradition. Fifty, the year of jubilee, was hallowed in Jewish tradition because it followed 49 years (mystic 7x7), and so was when debts should be forgiven, slaves freed and property returned. Shabuoth, the Feast of Weeks (on the Pentecostal 50th day) is similarly linked with seven because it follows the end of the seventh week after Passover. Sixty was used as the basis for the Chinese calendar. Seventy, the biblical life span, represented totality or universality. For many, 10,000 symbolized infinite numbers or infinite time. The Greeks called the 10,000 élite warriors of Persia, the "Immortals". A greater body of symbolism is attached to the numbers discussed below.

Zero

A relative latecomer to arithmetical calculation, zero soon took on symbolic meanings relating to the void, mystery, nothingness, death – but also eternity, the absolute or essence of reality, totality, the cosmic egg or womb, potentiality, the generative interval. Pythagoras saw the sign (known from Babylonia, but mathematically developed mainly in Arabia and India) as containing all things. It was the Tao, the begetter of one. In Mayan glyphs it was represented by the cosmic spiral. As the decimal multiplier, it has more recent associations with power.

One

A symbol of God in Islam and other monotheistic religions, the number one was an emblem of primordial unity. It could also stand for the sun or light, and the origin of life. In Western tradition, the Arabic numeral itself had phallic, aggressive and active symbolism. For the school of Pythagoras it was the point, the common basis for all calculation. It was the Confucian perfect entity, the indivisible, the mystic centre from which everything else radiated. More obviously, one is an emblem of beginning, of the self, and of loneliness.

Two

Two is symbolically the most ambivalent of all numbers, representing as it does the binary principle. It can stand for synthesis but also division, attraction and repulsion, equilibrium and conflict. Protective animal statues in the ancient world were often paired to symbolize strength. Yet in Chinese symbolism, two is an unlucky, weak (yin) number, lacking a centre. Double deities often stand for opposing principles or contrary aspects of a single deity, just as twins can symbolize doubled force or warring spirits of good and evil. Associated with the division of a primordial unity, two is linked with the female principle, union, love, fertility and growth, and the dynamics of creation and destruction.

Three

Three is the most positive number in symbolism as well as religious thought, legend, mythology, and folklore where the tradition of "third time lucky" is very old. The Christian doctrine of the Trinity, which enabled a monotheistic God to be worshipped through the Holy Spirit and the person of Christ, is an example of the way in which Three can replace One as the symbol of a more versatile and powerful unity. Three-headed or three-fold gods such as the Greek Hecate or the Celtic Brigit had multiple functions or controlled several spheres. Religious triads are common – the Hindu Trimurti of Brahma (creator), Vishnu (sustainer) and Shiva (destroyer); the three brothers, Zeus (Jupiter in Roman myth), Poseidon (Neptune) and Hades (Pluto), who controlled the Greek world with their triple attributes, the three-forked lightning, the trident and the three-headed dog Cerberus; the three great Inca deities of sun, moon and storm; and the three brothers who controlled the heavens in China. Other mythological and allegorical figures also frequently come in threes, such as the Fates, the Furies, the Graces, the Harpies, the Gorgons, or the Christian theological virtues of Faith, Hope and Charity. Three is a much repeated number in the New Testament: the three Magi; the three denials of Peter; the three crosses on Golgotha; the Resurrection after three days.

For Pythagoras, three was the number of harmony, for Aristotle, of completeness, because it had an end as well as a beginning and middle. Similarly, in Taoism, three symbolized strength because it implied a central element. In China, it was an auspicious number symbolizing sanctity, loyalty, respect and refinement. Three was the number of the Japanese sacred "treasures" – the mirror, sword and jewel. In Buddhism it was the number of holy scriptures, the Tripitaka. In Hinduism, it was the number of letters in the mystic word Om (*Aum*), expressing the rhythm of the whole cosmos and of divinity.

Three is, significantly, the number of a family unit, the smallest "tribe". In Africa it was the number of maleness (penis and testicles). In sexual relationships, it is an emblem of conflict – the eternal triangle. Otherwise, three is usually seen as a lucky number, possibly because it symbolizes the resolution of a conflict – a decisive action that may lead to success or disaster. In folk tales, wishes are customarily granted in threes. Heroes or heroines are allowed three choices, set three trials or given three chances to succeed. Ritual actions are often performed thrice, as in Islamic daily ablutions, in salutations or in making auguries. The usual graphic symbol of three is the triangle, but other triform symbols include the triskelion (a form of triple-armed swastika), the trefoil, the Chinese trigram, the trident, the fleur-de-lis, three fishes with a single head (the Christian Trinity) and three-legged lunar animals (phases of the moon).

Four

The symbolism of four is drawn primarily from the square and the four-armed cross. It stands for solidity, comprehensiveness, ubiquity, organization, power, intellect, justice and omnipotence. The square was the emblem of the earth in both India and China. The four-armed cross is the most common emblem of totality, the four directions of space. The significance of the four cardinal points, thought to be ruled by powerful gods of wind and weather, led to the dominance of the number four in religion and ritual throughout much of pre-Columbian America. The four heavenly gods of the Mayan pantheon, the four creator gods of the Aztecs, the four worlds of creation in the Hopi tradition of Arizona, all point to this fundamental theme. As a symbol of universality, four was hardly less important in celestial geography elsewhere. The concept of the four rivers that flow from the Tree of Life in paradise and bring the gift of spiritual nourishment or immortality is common to Babylonian, Iranian, Hindu, Christian, Teutonic, Nordic and Buddhist traditions. Four-faced gods such as Amun-Ra in Egypt and Brahma in India symbolize rulership of all elements.

Emblematic of terrestial order and universality, four was also the number of castes in Hindu society. The four letters YHVH outlined the unspeakable name of the Hebrew God. The 12 Tribes of Israel were grouped under four emblems: man, lion, bull and eagle. These became the Christian emblems of the four Evangelists Matthew, Mark, Luke and John. The many other fourfold symbols in the Bible, such as the four horsemen of the Apocalypse, similarly express the idea of universality.

Four was, in Pythagorean terms, the first number giving a solid – the tetrahedron with a base and three sides. Symbolizing the stabilizing force of religion, the square was the basis of much sacred architecture worldwide.

The world or heaven was thought to be supported by four pillars (Egypt) or giants (Central America). In the process of mummification in Egypt, four guardian-headed canopic jars held the entrails of the dead. A body lying in state is still conventionally watched over by four guards. As a "rational" number, four symbolized the intellect. In ancient Western tradition there were four elements – earth, air, fire and water – and four humours.

Five

Linked with humanity, five is often represented graphically by a man whose head and outstretched limbs form a five-pointed star, or by the pentagram, also called pentacle, drawn with lines crossing to the five points.

Apart from its emblematic association with the human microcosm (and the hand itself), the number five was an important symbol of totality in Chinese, Japanese, Celtic and other traditions which included the centre as a fifth direction of space. Other associations are with love, health, sensuality, meditation, analysis, criticism, strength, integration, organic growth and the heart.

According to Pythagorean mysticism, five, like seven, was a holistic number, marrying three (heaven) with the terrestrial two, and was fundamental both in nature and in art. It was linked in the classical world with Aphrodite (in Roman myth, Venus), the goddess of love and beauty. The association with love and sex may be based on the combination of the male number three with the female number two. Or it may derive from a more ancient Mesopotamian tradition in which the five-pointed star was an emblem of Ishtar whose planet was Venus, the primary evening star. In Mexico it was the Aztec god of the morning star, Quetzalcoatl, who was associated with the number five. He rose from the underworld (linked with five) on the fifth day, traditionally the day the first corn shoots appeared after sowing.

Extending the significance of this number, the Aztecs saw their own era as that of the "Fifth Sun". In India, the five-pointed star was an emblem of Shiva, sometimes shown with five faces. Five was a Japanese Buddhist emblem of perfection. In China, where five symbolized the centre, its significance was still greater: in addition to the five regions of space and five senses, there were said to be five elements, metals, colours, tones and tastes. In Christian iconography, five refers to the number of Christ's wounds. In Islam, it was a beneficial and protective number, the five fundamentals of religion being faith, prayer, fasting, pilgrimage and charity. Five was a symbol of strength in Judaism, and the number of the quintessence in alchemy.

Six

Six symbolizes union and equilibrium, graphically expressed by the hexagram combining two triangles, one pointing up (male, fire, heaven), one pointing down (female, water, earth). This figure, now known as the Star of David, symbolized the union of Israel and Judah and is also taken as an ideogram for the human soul.

The Chinese oracular Book of Changes, the *I Ching* (see pages 162–3), is based on the unifying symbolism of six broken or unbroken lines making up an overall system of 64 linear "hexagrams". In the Pythagorean system, six represented chance or luck – as it does in modern dice. As the cube with six surfaces, the number represents stability and truth. In Genesis, and in earlier Sumerian-Semitic tradition, the world was created in six days. According to the book of Revelation (13:18), the number of the Beast (Satan) was "666". One theory is that this number was chosen because it falls repeatedly short of the sacred number seven; other numerological theories explain it as a coded version of the name of various oppressive Roman emperors. Alternatively, it is suggested as a monastic number that identifies Simon Magus, a forerunner of Gnosticism, whom the writer of Revelation may have regarded as a dangerous influence in early Christianity.

Seven

A sacred, mystical and magic number, especially in the traditions of western Asia, seven symbolizes cosmic and spiritual order and the completion of a natural cycle. Its importance is based on early astronomy – especially the seven wandering stars or dynamic celestial bodies (the sun and moon, Mars,

Mercury, Jupiter, Venus, and Saturn) after which the days of the week in many cultures were named. Another influence was the four seven-day phases of the moon that made up the 28 days of the lunar calendar. Arithmeticians further noted that the first seven digits added together came to 28.

Seven was fundamental in the Mesopotamian world, which divided both the earth and heaven into seven zones and depicted the Tree of Life with seven branches. In the Bible, God's blessing on the seventh day is followed by scores of other references to seven. It was the number of Jewish feasts, festivals, purifications and years between sabbaticals. There were seven Pillars of Wisdom and in other cultures the number was often linked with intellectual mastery. Seven was sacred to the god Osiris in Egypt (a symbol of immortality); to the god Apollo in Greece (the number of strings on his lyre); to Mithras, the Persian god of light (the number of initiatory stages in his cult); and to the Buddha (his seven emblems).

In Hindu tradition, the world mountain has seven faces, the sun seven rays. The seventh ray is a symbol of the centre, the power of God. In Islam, where the number seven symbolizes perfection, there are seven heavens, earths, seas, hells and doors to paradise. Pilgrims walk around the sacred Kaaba at Mecca seven times. Seven had protective power in Arabic and other folklore customs and was associated particularly with childbirth.

Eight

Spatially eight is an emblem of cosmic equilibrium, and cyclically the symbol of renewal, rebirth or beatitude. The octagon was seen as a form mediating between the square and circle, combining stability with totality. Adding to its symbolism of totality, the number eight represented the four cardinal points and their four intermediate points. Celtic, Hindu and many other iconographic wheels were eight-armed – as is Vishnu in Hindu art. Baptismal fonts in the shape of octagons also incorporate the symbolism of renewal derived from the fact that eight follows the symbolic "complete" number, seven, and begins a new cycle. Eight was a lucky number in China, where there were eight Taoist Immortals, and also in Japanese Shintoism. The lotus is often shown with eight petals – the number of chakras and of Buddhist symbols of good augury.

The shape of the arabic numeral "8" was equated with the caduceus, and eight is the number of the Greek god Hermes (in Egyptian myth, Thoth) in Hermetic magic. The Star of Bethlehem is often shown with eight points.

Nine

As the triple triad, nine is a supremely powerful number in most traditions, notably in China, in Buddhism and in the Celtic world. The most auspicious Chinese number and most potent yang number, it was the basis of much Taoist ceremonial and ritual divisions in architecture and property. In mysticism it represented the triple synthesis of mind, body and spirit, or of the underworld, earth and heaven.

The number was a Hebrew symbol of truth and a Christian symbol of order within order – hence the organization of angels into nine choirs. There were nine celestial spheres in many traditions and, in Central America, nine underworlds. Often linked with male courage or endurance, nine was a key number in the shamanistic rituals of northern and central Asia. The nine days and nights during which the Nordic god Odin (Woden in Teutonic tradition) hanged himself on the World Tree Yggdrasil symbolized the ritual period required for his magical resurrection or rejuvenation.

Ten

Ten is a symbol of perfection – the mystical number of completion and unity, especially in Jewish tradition; hence the number of the Commandments revealed to Moses by God, summarizing the most important Hebrew religious obligations.

In the Pythagorean system, ten was a symbol of the whole of creation, represented by a star of ten points, the holy tetraktys – the sum of the first four numbers. As the number of digits on the human hands, ten was a symbol of completeness even on the simplest level. The ancient Egyptians based their calendar on the decans, 36 bright stars divided by intervals of ten days. Each decan was thought to affect human life – a significant concept in the development of Greek astrology.

A tenth was almost universally the percentage of spoils, property or produce owed to a god or king in the ancient world – the basis of the tithes system. In China, ten was the perfectly balanced number, represented by a cross with a short central bar. As a combination of male and female numerals, it was a symbol of marriage. The decade symbolizes a turning point in history or a cycle in myth, as in the Fall of Troy after a ten-year siege.

Eleven

Eleven is associated by St Augustine with sin, for the rather sophisticated reason that it suggested excess – being one more than the perfect 10 – and it was a number also linked with danger, conflict or rebellion. In Europe, it was sometimes known as the "Devil's dozen"; but African shamans used 11 as a number propitious to fecundity. Being saved at the "eleventh hour" alludes to Christ's parable of the labourers who received a day's wage even though they had been hired in the last hour of the working day.

Twelve

The base number of space and time in astrology, ancient astronomy and calendric science, twelve gained great symbolic importance, especially in Judeo-Christian tradition where it was the number of the chosen. It represented cosmic organization, zones of celestial influence, and an achieved cycle of time (the 12 calendar months, 12 hours of day and night, 12 groups of years in China). As the product of the two powerful numbers three and four, it symbolized a union of spiritual and temporal planes. In the Bible, 12 is the number of the sons of Jacob, and therefore of the tribes of Israel, the jewels in the priest's breastplate, major disciples of Christ, fruits of the Tree of Life, gates of the Holy City and stars in the crown of Mary. Twelve was also the number of disciples of Mithras and, for some Muslims, the number of descendants of the prophet Ali. Solar astrology was based upon the movement of the sun through the twelve signs of the zodiac.

The Greek author Hesiod (*c.*700BC) said that there were 12 Titans, and in later Greek tradition 12 gods ruled Olympus. There were also 12 prominent Knights of the Round Table. Calendric symbolism underlies the 12 days of Christmas, a tradition developed from the period of Yuletide and Saturnalia festivity at the December solstice – a day representing each coming month.

Thirteen

The tradition that thirteen is an unlucky number appears to be associated with the problems of early lunar-based calendars which needed the intercalation of a 13th "month", thought to be unfavourable. Advice not to sow crops on the 13th of any month goes back at least to the Greek writer Hesiod (*c.*700BC). Satan was said to be the "13th figure" at witch's rites, and in the Tarot, Death is the 13th card of the *major arcana*. However, in Central America, the number 13 was held to be sacred because there were 13-day weeks in the religious calendar.

Forty

The last number carrying major symbolic weight is 40. It was used ritually in Judeo-Christian and Islamic tradition to define significant periods of time – especially spiritual preparation or testing, purification, penance, waiting or fasting. One plausible explanation for the choice of this number is that Babylonian astronomers associated natural catastrophes, particularly storms and floods, with a 40-day period in spring when the Pleiades cluster of stars disappeared. Another is the ancient idea that the dead took 40 days to entirely fade away. Roman funerary banquets were held after 40 days. The idea that 40 days was a suitably long period for purification led the port of Marseilles to impose a 40-day port ban (the quarantine) on ships from plague countries in the 14th century.

Early historians used 40 more as a symbolic number than as an accurate one. Thus, in the Bible, the Flood lasted 40 days and nights; the Israelites wandered 40 years in the wilderness; Moses listened to God for 40 days and nights on Mount Sinai; David and Solomon each ruled for 40 years; Christ spent 40 days fasting in the wilderness (now Lent), 40 months preaching, and 40 days after Easter he ascended to heaven. In Egypt, Osiris disappeared for 40 days, the period of religious fasting. Muhammad received the word of God at the age of 40. Many other Hebrew and Islamic rituals testify to the power of 40 as a number symbolic of accomplishment or change.

ALCHEMY

Alchemy is commonly viewed as a pseudo-science concerned with the transformation of base metals into gold: its status is that of a curiosity, notable for the contributions of its practitioners to the emerging discipline of chemistry. This misconception is understandable given the shroud of secrecy deliberately drawn over the true goal of alchemy – the attainment of enlightenment. At the most esoteric level, the base metal of the alchemist was symbolic of the unredeemed self, while the gold, with its capacity to shine and its incorruptible nature, was symbolic of the transformed spiritual self. The intention was to turn the dross of everyday thought and experience into a pure, spiritual state.

The symbolism of alchemical transformation was used to disguise what the powerful medieval European Church condemned as an heretical practice, since it was based upon the belief that the individual could raise himself or herself toward salvation without the agency of established religion.

However, alchemy was more than just a symbol of inner transformation: it provided the means by which this could be achieved. Alchemists aimed to transmute the base material into the "philosopher's stone", also known as the Elixir or Tincture. Turning base metals into gold was proof of its power, but the elixir was an aim in itself, an essence rather than merely an agent. The journey to enlightenment – known to alchemists as the Great Work – had interdependent physical and spiritual dimensions.

Theory and practice

Alchemy is thought to have originated in ancient Egypt, and to have been part of the esoteric wisdom of the Greeks, Arabs, Indians and Chinese. The first alchemical text to appear in western Europe was the 12th-century translation into Latin by an Englishman, Robert of

Chester, of the Arabic *Book of the Composition of Alchemy*. The theory underlying alchemical practice derives from the ancient world-view in which the whole of reality, including mankind, is created from a non-physical *materia prima* (first matter) – the universal magical element – that takes form as the elements earth, fire, air and water. Because these elements can be transformed into one another, it is apparent that all material things are based upon the principle of change.

According to this world-view, it was possible to transform a substance back into the *materia prima*, and conversely the *materia prima* could be returned to the world in a different form.

The practice of alchemy is laid out in medieval texts so obscure and loaded with symbolism as to be nearly incomprehensible. Some scholars argue that in defying conventional logic, these texts test the resolve of the seeker, who must rely on inspiration and intuition to guide him on the path to enlightenment. More cynical commentators hold that the tortuous texts merely conceal a fraud. However, it is clear that the alchemist begins the Great Work with the *materia prima*, which it is claimed one must mine for oneself, and which takes the form of a "stone" (not to be confused with the philosopher's stone itself). This stone, of which the exact nature is not revealed, is pulverized and mixed with a "first agent", enigmatically described as "dry water" or as "fire without flame", which some alchemists suggest is prepared by a secret process from cream of tartar. The amalgam of these two substances is moistened with dew and placed in a sealed vessel or "philosopher's egg", and heated at high temperature over a long time.

During incubation, the two principles within the *materia prima*, usually referred to symbolically as "sulphur" (red, male, solar, hot energy) and "mercury" (white, female, lunar, cold energy) are said to fight venomously, each eventually slaying the other and producing a black putrefaction, the *nigredo*, the "black of blacks". This completes the first stage of the Great Work.

In the second stage, the blackness becomes overlaid with rainbow colours (sometimes depicted as a peacock tail or pearl), which are in turn covered by a whiteness, the *albedo*. At this point, the two principles of the *materia prima* reappear in a new form, as the "red king" (Sulphur of the Wise) emerges from the womb of the "white queen" (mercury, or the White Rose). King and Queen are united in the fire of love. From their union comes perfection, the philosopher's stone, the catalyst capable of transmuting base metals into gold and the key to spiritual enlightenment.

For the alchemist, correct motivation was essential in undertaking the Great Work. The quest of those who concentrated merely on the chemical processes was doomed to fail. If the seeker was driven by greed, then, as one alchemical text puts it, he would "reap but smoke".

The original "stone", which the seeker must mine for himself, symbolizes the deep inner longing to find our true spiritual nature, known to alchemists as the "active principle". The "first agent" stands for the "passive principle", the indwelling energy of which most of us are unaware as we travel through life, but which carries the potential for spiritual growth. Once contact is made between the active and passive principles within the "furnace" of deep meditation, a struggle ensues as the active principle, used to obtaining what it wants through the exercise of the will, finds that the passive principle cannot be vanquished in this way. There follows the dark night of the soul of which mystics speak, in which both active and passive principles seem to have been annihilated and the individual feels utterly forsaken. Out of this despair, however, arises the rainbow revelation that love and not force is required, and this is followed by the union of the two principles, the red king and the white queen, whose progeny is born of water and the spirit.

What were the actual spiritual practices behind this symbolic process? Meditating upon the alchemical symbols themselves, in a progression through each of the stages, was certainly involved. But a Chinese alchemical text, *The Secret of the Golden Flower*, gives us further clues. It tells us how, through meditation, physical energy can be visualized as gathering and concentrating in the lower body, in the "place of power" below the navel, where it generates immense heat and then (symbolically) passes "the boiling point [and] mounts upwards like flying snow ... to the summit of the Creative". Perhaps, for all their archaic and obscure language, the alchemists (or at least a few among them) did indeed effect the union of the red king and the white queen, and raised the base metal of the physical being into the pure gold of the greater spiritual self.

THE CABBALA

The Cabbala is an extraordinary system of theoretical and practical wisdom designed to provide its students not only with a path of mental and spiritual growth but also with a symbolic map of creation itself. Rooted in 3rd-century mysticism, the Cabbala developed in an essentially Hebrew tradition, and the earliest known Cabbalistic text, the *Sefer Yetzira*, appeared sometime between the 3rd and 6th centuries. The powerful appeal of the system led to its incorporation into certain aspects of Christian thinking in the 15th century. The Italian scholar Giovanni Pico della Mirandola argued that "no science can better convince us of the divinity of Jesus Christ than magic and the Cabbala".

Working with symbols

Essentially, the Cabbala is an esoteric teaching centred on a system of symbols, which are held to reflect the mystery of God and the universe, and for which the Cabbalist must find the key. At the theoretical level, these keys allow him (the Cabbalist has traditionally been male) to understand the spiritual dimensions of the universe, while at the practical level they allow him to use the powers associated with these dimensions for magical purposes (that is for the processes of physical, psychological or spiritual transformation). The keys to the Cabbala lie hidden in the meaning of the divine revelations which make up the holy scriptures: just as God is hidden, so too are the inner secrets of his divine message. These secrets are revealed by decoding the scriptures via a system of equivalences or *gematria*, in which each letter of the Hebrew alphabet has a number associated with it, or can be permutated or abbreviated in certain ways. For example, the brass serpent constructed by Moses and set on a pole so that "if a serpent had bitten any man, when he beheld the serpent of brass he lived" (Numbers 21:9) is converted through *gematria* to the number 358, which is also the numerical equivalent of the word "Messiah". Thus, the brass serpent is held to be a prophecy of the coming of the Messiah, who will save all those bitten by the longing for spiritual truth. This led Christian Cabbalists to adopt the symbol of the serpent on the cross to represent Christ.

So extensive are the possibilities for *gematria* that an understanding of Hebrew is necessary in order to study the Cabbala. In the past, Cabbalists insisted on a number of further stringent conditions before accepting students: they had to lead morally pure lives, have great powers of concentration and be completely dedicated to the task. For this reason, the Cabbala is known to most people only in its most accessible form – the *sefiroth*, "secret writings" or trees of life. But despite their apparent simplicity, the *sefiroth* are a powerful and all-encompassing symbol.

The sefiroth

In its basic interpretation, the *sefiroth* explains creation. The reason for existence is held to be that God wished to behold himself: to accomplish this, he withdrew his presence – the Absolute All – from one place so that he could "gaze upon his own face". In the act of calling the universe into being, God revealed ten of his attributes, each of which is represented in the *sefiroth* by a *sefirah*. Each *sefirah* is linked to another in a set of precise relationships: the path begins at *keter* (the crown) which denotes all that was, is and will be, and leads eventually to *malkhut* (the kingdom) which corresponds to the presence of God in matter. The direction of the path from *keter* to *malkhut*, through the attributes of wisdom, understanding, mercy, judgment, beauty, eternity, reverberation and foundation, is governed by the three Divine Principles of Will, Mercy and Justice. In most visualizations of the *sefiroth*, the path takes the form of a zigzag or lightning flash as the three divine principles, associated with balance (Will), expansion (Mercy) and constraint (Justice), operate in turn.

Although all the laws relating to being and creation are embedded within the *sefiroth*, they exist as unrealized plans. In order to account for the many manifestations of God, the Cabbala contains the concept of the Four Worlds or cosmic cycles, each of which has its own tree of life. The Four Worlds – Manifestation, Creation, Formation and Action – can be seen as the different aspects of God through which the universe was brought into being. They refer also to the hierarchy of the Worlds revealed to the 6th-century-BC prophet Ezekiel who, in a vision, saw the likeness of the glory of God (Manifestation) on a throne (Creation), riding in a chariot (Formation) above the world (Action). Each world possesses all the characteristics of the one above, and so is more complex and subject to more laws. The Four Worlds are usually depicted as four interlocking *sefiroth* – the extended tree of life.

The patterns and relationships enshrined in the *sefiroth* are fundamental to being and can therefore be applied to all areas of endeavour. Properly used and understood, the *sefiroth* are a blueprint from which all phenomena – cosmic and human – can be explained and ultimately controlled.

The Cabbala is essentially an oral tradition; the initiate is guided by an experienced mentor who stands in for the student's imperfectly developed consciousness and steers him away from danger. The initiate usually starts by studying each *sefirah* of the ten, ascending the tree towards full enlightenment. Each *sefirah* represents an aspect of the self that must be fully developed before the student can proceed to the stages that lie beyond. Once in possession of a theoretical understanding of each *sefirah*, the Cabbalist, through further study and meditation, and by learning how the tasks associated with the twenty-two paths between the individual *sefirah* can assist his progress, is able to begin his ascent through the tree. This may form his life's work and few reach the end of it, but once completed he can move beyond symbolism to experience infinity itself.

Further Reading

Boardman, J., Griffin, J. and Murray, O. *Oxford History of Greece and the Hellenistic World*, Oxford University Press, Oxford (UK), and New York (US), 2001

Carter, G. (compiler). *The Illustrated Guide to Latin American Mythology*, Studio Editions Ltd., London (UK), 1995

Chamberlain, J. *Chinese Gods*, Pelanduk Publications, Selangor, Malaysia, 1987

Cohen, D. *The Secret Language of the Mind*, Duncan Baird Publishers, London (UK), and Chronicle Books, San Francisco (US), 1996

Cornelius, G. and Devereux, P. *The Language of Stars & Planets: A Visual Key to Celestial Mysteries*, Duncan Baird Publishers, London (UK), and Chronicle Books, San Francisco (US), 2003

Fontana, D. *The Language of Symbols: A Visual Key to Symbols and their Meanings*, Duncan Baird Publishers, London (UK), 2003, and Chronicle Books, San Francisco (US), 1994

Gettings, F. *The Arkana Dictionary of Astrology*, Arkana, Penguin Group, London (UK), and New York (US), 1990

Green, M.J. *Dictionary of Celtic Myth and Legend*, Thames and Hudson Ltd, London (UK), and New York (US), 1992

Hope, J. *The Language of the Spirit: A Visual Key to Enlightenment and Destiny*, Duncan Baird Publishers, London (UK), and Chronicle Books, San Francisco (US), 2003

Miller, M. and Taube, K. *The Gods and Symbols of Ancient Mexico and the Maya*, Thames and Hudson Ltd, London (UK), and New York (US), 1993

Saunders, N.J. *Animal Spirits*, Duncan Baird Publishers, London (UK), and Little, Brown & Company Inc., Boston, MA (US), 1995

Tresidder, J. *1001 Symbols*, Duncan Baird Publishers, London (UK), and Chronicle Books, San Francisco (US), 2003

Tresidder, J. (general editor). *The Complete Dictionary of Symbols in Myth, Art and Literature*, Duncan Baird Publishers, London (UK), and Chronicle Books, San Francisco (US), 2004

Vitebsky, P. *The Shaman*, Duncan Baird Publishers, London (UK), and Little, Brown & Company Inc., Boston, MA (US), 2000

Willis, R. (general editor). *World Mythology*, Duncan Baird Publishers, London (UK), and Oxford University Press, New York (US), 2006

Waterstone, R. *India*, Duncan Baird Publishers, London (UK), and Thorsons USA, 2002

Zimmerman, L.J and Molyneaux, B.L. *Native North America*, Duncan Baird Publishers, London (UK), and Little, Brown & Company Inc., Boston, MA (US), 2002

Index

Page numbers in **bold** indicate main entries. Page numbers in *italic* relate to captions.

Picture Credits

The author and publishers would like to thank the following people, museums and photographic libraries for permission to reproduce their material. Every care has been taken to trace copyright owners. However, if we have omitted anyone we apologise and will, if informed, make corrections in any further edition.

Key:
BAL Bridgeman Art Library, London
ET e.t. archive, London
MH Michael Holford, Loughton, Essex
WFA Werner Forman Archive, London

Page **The Spirit Incarnate**
1 British Museum, London (MH)
2 Oriental Museum, Durham University (BAL)
7 Staatsbibliothek, Berlin (AKG, London)
8–9 Hoysaleswara Temple, Halebid, India (Dinodia Picture Agency, Bombay/BAL)
10 Private Collection (The Stapleton Collection/BAL)
11 Horniman Museum, London
12 British Museum, London (MH)
13 Sandro Botticelli: The Birth of Venus, *c.*1485. Uffizi, Florence (BAL)
14 Danish School: Execution of Louis XVI, 1793. Musee Carnavalet, Paris (ET)
15 Leonardo da Vinci: Vitruvian Man, *c.*1492., *detail.* Galleria dell'Accademia, Venice (BAL)
16 Masaccio (1401–28): Adam and Eve banished from Paradise. Brancacci Chapel, Santa Maria del Carmine, Florence (BAL)
17 Victoria & Albert Museum, London (MH)
18 Images, London
19 Giotto (*c.*1266–1337): St Mary Magdalene, *detail.* Duomo. Florence (BAL)
20 Studio of Giovanni-Battista Tiepolo (1696–1770): St Augustine, St Louis of France. St John the Evangelist and a Bishop Saint. York City Art Gallery (BAL)
21 Museum fur Volkerkunde, Berlin (WFA)
22 Andrea Previtali (active 1502–1528): Salvator Mundi. National Gallery, London
23 Tariq Rajab Museum (Images, London)
24t Les Trois Freres Cave, Magdalena, Pyrenees (AKG, London)
24b British Museum, London
25 Pieter Brueghel the Elder: The Triumph of Death, *c.*1562. Prado, Madrid (BAL)

Soul, Mind, and the Supernatural
26–7 William Blake: The Angel Michael binding Satan, *c.*1800., *detail.* Fogg Art Museum, Harvard University, Cambridge, MA., gift of W.A White (BAL)
28 Joachim Patenir (1480–1524): Charon crossing the River Styx. Prado, Madrid (ET)
29 Guariento di Arpo (*c.*1338-77): The Archangel Michael. Museo Civico, Padua (BAL)
30 William Blake: Glad Day or The Dance of Albion, *c.*1794. British Museum, London (BAL)
31 Iraq Museum, Baghdad (Erich Lessing / AKG, London)
32 Statens Historiska Museet, Stockholm (WFA)
33 Eric Lawson / Hutchison Library, London
34t R.Ian Lloyd / Hutchison Library, London
34b Wallpainting from the Columbarium in the Villa Pamphili, Rome. *c.*1st century AD. British Museum, London (MH)
35 British Museum, London (MH)
37 Pietro Perugino : The Marriage of the Virgin, 1500–04. Musee des Beaux Arts, Caen (Giraudon/BAL)
38 Bibliotheque Nationale, Paris (AKG, London)
39 British Museum, London (WFA)
40 Leonardo da Vinci: Cecilia Gallerani (Lady with the Ermine), c1490. Czartorysky Museum, Cracow (ET)
41 Hieronymus Bosch (*c.*1450–1516): The Table of the Seven Deadly Sins. *detail.* Prado, Madrid (BAL)

The Animal World
42–3 Images, London
44 Staatliche Antikenslg. & Glyptothek, Munich (Erich Lessing / AKG, London)
45 Smithsonian Institution, Washington D.C. (BAL)
46 Master of the House Book (active *c.*1475–1490): Adoration of the Shepherds. Alte Pinatothek, Munich (AKG, London)
47 British Museum, London (MH)
48 Royal Library, Copenhagen (BAL)
49 Henry Fuseli: Titania Awakes, 1793–4. Kunsthaus, Zurich. (BAL)
51t Vitlycke, Sweden (WFA)
51b The Egyptian Museum, Cairo (WFA)
52t Philip Goldman Collection, London (WFA)
52b Edward Burne-Jones: Garden of the Hesperides, 1870–73. Private Collection (BAL)
53 British Museum, London (AKG London)
54–5 Raphael: St George and the Dragon, *c.*1505. Louvre, Paris (BAL)
56 Private Collection (Dinodia Picture Agency, Bombay /BAL)
57 Statens Historiska Museet, Stockholm (WFA)
58 Philip Goldman Collection, London (WFA)
59t Mexican National Library, Mexico City (WFA)
59b British Museum, London
60 British Museum, London (BAL)
61 Anne Girodet-Trioson: The ghosts of French warriors being brought before Ossian by Victory, *c.*1800. Chateau de Malmaison, Paris (Lauros-Giraudon/BAL)
62 Andrea Lilio: St Roch, 1596. Galleria Nationale Marche, Urbino (ET)
63 Attrib. David Ryckaert III (1612–61): Gates of Hades. *detail.* Johnny van Haeften Gallery, London (BAL)
64 Bibliotheque Nationale, Paris (AKG, London)
65 Frogs, from *Beautyway – A Navaho Ceremonia*, pub lished by Bellingen Foundation, 1957.
66 Pergamon Museum, Berlin (Erich Lessing / AKG, London)
67 Nikolaus of Verdun: Jonah in the stomach of the Sea Monster, detail from the Verdun Altar, 1181. Stifkskirche Klosterneuburg, Austria (Erich Lessing / AKG, London)
68 Lucas Cranach the Elder (1472–1553): The Trinity. Museum der Bildenden Kunste, Leipzig (AKG, London)
69 Private Collection (Jean-Louis Nou / AKG, London)
70 Jean-Louis-Cesar Lair (1781-1828): The Torture of Prometheus. Musee Crozatier, Le Puy-en-Velay (Giraudon/BAL)
71 Royal Library, Copenhagen (BAL)
72 Private Collection (MH)
73 Geese fresco from pyramid of Meifum, 4th Dynasty. Egyptian Museum, Cairo (E.T)

The Plant Kingdom
74–5 Master of Oberrheinischer: Garden of Paradise, *c.*1410. *detail.* Stadelsches Kunstinstitut, Frankfurt-am-Main (BAL)
76 Victoria & Albert Museum, London (ET)
77 British Museum, London
78 Jean Auguste Dominique Ingres: Study of Victory for the Apothesis of Homer, 1826–27. Musee Bonnat, Bayonne (Bulloz/BAL)

79 Private Collection (BAL)
80 Eitan Simanor/Axiom, London
81 Wellcome Museum, London (MH)
82 Rogier van der Weyden: Branch of Holly, pre. 1437. Courtauld Gallery, London (BAL)
83 Fu Pao-Shih: The Seven Sages of the bamboo grove, early 20th century. Private Collection (BAL)
84 Jan Brueghel the Elder (1568–1625): A fantastic cave with Odysseus and Calypso. Johnny van Haeften Gallery, London (BAL)
85 Biblioteca Estense Modena (ET)
87 Michelangelo da Caravaggio: The Young Bacchus, *c.*1589., *detail.* Uffizi, Florence (BAL)
88 Joachim Utewael: The Judgement of Paris, 1615. National Gallery, London (BAL)
89 Dante Gabriel Rossetti: Proserpine, 1882. Birmingham Museum & Art Gallery (BAL)
90 Zimmermann Family Collection (AKG, London)
91 J. le Moyne de Morgues: Corn Poppy, *c.*1568. Victoria & Albert Museum, London (BAL)
92 British Library, London
93 John William Waterhouse: Echo and Narcissus, 1903. Walker Art Gallery, Liverpool. Board of Trustees: National Museums & Galleries on Merseyside (BAL)
94 Domenico Veneziano: The Annunciation, *c.*1445. Fitzwilliam Museum, University of Cambridge (BAL)
95 Bibliotheque Nationale, Paris (BAL)

Spirits of the Cosmos

96–7 Private Collection
98 The Three Magi, mosaic. S. Apollinare Nuovo, Ravenna (Scala, Florence)
99 Biblioteca Estense, Modena (ET)
100 British Museum, London (MH)
101 Louvre, Paris (BAL)
102 Louvre, Paris (AKG, London / Erich Lessing)
103 Private Collection (Bonhams, London/BAL)
104 Ambrogio Lorenzetti: Allegory of Good Government, *detail*, 1338–40. Palazzo Publico, Siena (ET)
105 Walter Crane (1845–915): The Seasons, Roy Miles Gallery, London (BAL)
106 Jan Cossiers (1600–71): Prometheus carrying fire. Prado, Madrid (BAL)
107 Royal Geographical Society, London (BAL)
108 Museum of Anthropology, University of British Columbia, Vancouver (WFA)
109 Private Collection (WFA)
110 Schindler Collection, New York (WFA)
111 Gustav Klimt: Danae, 1907–8. Private Collection (BAL)
112t D Shaw / Axiom, London
112b Musee Conde, Chantilly (Giraudon/BAL)
113 Victoria & Albert Museum, London (BAL)
114 Louis Joseph Watteau: The Temptation of St Anthony, 1781. Louvre, Paris (Giraudon/BAL)
115 Geoff Renner / Robert Harding Picture Library, London
116 Adina Tovy / Robert Harding Picture Library, London
117 Edward Lear (1812–88): Mount Sinai, *detail*, Private Collection (Christie's Images, London/BAL)
118 British Museum, London (BAL)
119 Fragment of wall painting from the tomb chapel of Sobekhotep: Nubians giving gold to Pharoah. British Museum, London
120 Gustave Moreau (1826–98): Salome, Armand Hammer Foundation, USA (BAL)
121t Haiphong Museum, Vietnam (WFA)
121b Bonhams, London (BAL)

Arts and Artefacts

122–3 Ian Cumming / Axiom, London
124 Jim Holmes / Axiom, London
125 Martin van Walckenborch (1535–1612): The Building of the Tower of Babel. Towneley Hall Art Gallery and Museum, Burnley, Lancashire (BAL)
126 British Library, London
127 Arcangelo di Cola da Camerino (fl.1416–21): The Martyrdom of St John the Evangelist. Galleria Estense, Modena (BAL)
128 Civic Library, Padua (ET)
129 Gherardo: The Combat of Love and Chastity, *c.*1475–1500. National Gallery, London
130 British Library, London (ET)
131 Ashmolean Museum, Oxford (BAL)
132t Turkish and Islamic Art Museum, Istanbul (ET)
132b British Museum, London
133 British Library, London(BAL)
134 Bonaventura Bellinghieri (*b.*1205): St Francis of Assisi. San Francesco, Pescia (ET)
135t Eugene Delacroix: Liberty Leading the People, detail, 1830. Louvre, Paris (BAL)
135b The Egyptian Museum, Cairo (WFA)
136 Noh Theatre Collection, Congo School, Kyoto (WFA)
137 Private Collection (WFA)
138 National Museum of Man, Ottawa (WFA)
139 Anon: Tsar Alexis of Russia, 17th century. Gripsholm Castle, Sweden (ET)
140 Victoria & Albert Museum, London
141 Museo di San Marco dell' Angelico, Florence (BAL)

Patterns and Graphics

142–3 Private Collection (Christie's Images, London/BAL)
144 Private Collection (ET)
145 Gottfried Lindauer(1839–1926): Tamati Waka Nene. Auckland City Art Gallery, New Zealand (BAL)
146 Prado, Madrid (ET)
147 Edfou, Egypt (MH)
148 Images, London
149 Mohamed Amin / Robert Harding Picture Library, London
150 Altarfront from Sindbjerg: Christ blessing, 1175–1200. National Museum of Copenhagen (ET)
151 British Museum, London
152 Khirbat Al-Mafjar, Jordan (BAL)
153 Ceiling of the room of the Labyrinth. Palazzo Ducale, Mantua (Scala, Florence)
154 Baptistery of Orthodox, Ravenna (ET)
155 Chester Beatty Library and Gallery of Oriental Art, Dublin (BAL)
156 Giovanni Battsita Carlone(1592–1677): Juno and Mars. Fitzwilliam Museum, Univerisity of Cambridge (BAL)
157t French School: The Black Virgin given to Louis XV, 18th century Musee Crozatier, Le Puy-en-Velay (Giraudon/BAL)
157b Victoria & Albert Museum, London (BAL)
158t Images, London
158b British Library, London (BAL)
159 Jimmy Holmes / Axiom, London

Symbol Systems

160 Zuccaro: Zodiac ceiling, *detail.* Palazzo Farnese, Caprarola (Scala, Florence)